Snowshoe Cats

Snowshoe Cats Owner's Manual

Snowshoe Cats care, personality, grooming, health and feeding all included.

by

Harvey Hendisson

Table of Contents

Chapter 1: Introduction

The Snowshoe breed has been with us since the 1960s and was officially recognized by associations and registries just over a decade ago. It is also a robust and healthy breed with a strong following all over the world. However, due to the challenges inherent in the breeding process, the Snowshoe is still a rare breed.

These lovely cats are ideal companions thanks to their charming personalities and temperaments. They are relaxed, sweet tempered, energetic, intelligent, playful and adaptable cats that are easy to train. The Snowshoe is also a very affectionate breed that requires more attention than many cats do. They don't do well if left alone for long periods of time.

They are good with children and get on well with other cats and with cat-friendly dogs. In a typical household they will be friendly to everyone, but will usually devote themselves almost entirely to one person. They are also ideal indoor cats.

Please note that some of the information in this book is not specific to the Snowshoe but can be applied to all cats. However, much of the details and tips are breed specific. I hope you find this book useful and fun to read.

Chapter 2: The history of the Snowshoe Cat

1) The history and origin of the Snowshoe cat

The Snowshoe is one of the breeds that originated in America. Like some other breeds, the origin of these beautiful cats lies in a happy accident of birth in the 1960s. A Siamese cat breeder in Philadelphia, Pennsylvania by the name of Dorothy Hinds-Daugherty had a cat that gave birth to a litter of kittens. Three of them had unique markings: white points and white feet. Hinds-Daugherty was intrigued by these kittens and her quest for a new breed began.

She began the Snowshoe breeding program using seal point Siamese and bicolour American Shorthairs. The resulting offspring of these breeds lacked the Siamese points. However, by breeding the offspring with Siamese the desired look was achieved. The breed was named the Snowshoe because of their white feet.

Hinds-Daugherty later abandoned the breeding program and it was taken over by Vikki Olander. It was Olander who wrote the standard for the breed and began the long process of getting the Snowshoe recognised by cat associations and federations. By 1977 she was the only breeder in the United States and was battling to maintain the program. A call from Jim Hoffman and Georgia Kuhnell, who were both interested in the breed, changed all that. By the time Olander was no longer involved, the breed had a loyal and strong following.

1986 saw the start of the committed and successful Snowshoe breeding program in the United Kingdom. But, two short years later Maureen Shackell was the only breeder left. Fortunately, she was joined by Mollie Southall. Jointly, they only had five cats with which to save the breed. Southall's imported her senior breeding male, *Ferry Vom Friedwald*, from Germany. He introduced a much needed new bloodline to the program. The gene pool for the breed was further widened in 2006 when Kelly Cruise joined the group and brought new colours, such as apricot, and patterns to the Snowshoe breed.

In terms of current breeding, associations and federations allow Snowshoes to be outcrossed to Siamese, Oriental Shorthairs and American Shorthairs.

2) *The status of the breed*

The Snowshoe is still a rare breed. The primary reason for this is the difficulty with breeding cats that conform to the exacting breed standards. This inconsistency is thanks to a complex mix of recessive and other genes, which are hard to control.

For instance, the "V" facial pattern is created by a gene of incomplete dominance. In other words, if a kitten has two dominant genes the facial feature will be too large. A kitten with only one of these genes the marking will be smaller. The white feet or boots that are so characteristic of the Snowshoe can arise as a result of either a gloving gene or a piebalding gene. The fact that both of these are a challenge to control mean that the white may be too far up or down on the leg or foot, the boots might not match or one leg or foot may not have a white boot or shoe at all.

Despite the difficulties, the Snowshoe attained championship status with the American Cat Fanciers Association (AFCA) in 1990, The International Cat Association (TICA) in 1993, and the UK's The Governing Council of the Cat Fancy (GCCF) in 2013. In addition, the breed is fully recognized by the Fédération Internationale Féline in France and the American Association of Cat Enthusiasts.

Chapter 3: General information about the Snowshoe

1) The Snowshoe's personality

The Snowshoe's personality makes it an ideal pet because these cats are sweet and even tempered, playful, very affectionate and loving, active and playful, relaxed, and sociable.

They enjoy human company a great deal, although they can be a little shy with strangers, and they are good with children. These cats also get on well with other cats and with cat-friendly dogs. Snowshoes do, however, usually bond with one family member more than with any other and will usually stick close to this person.

This affectionate, social nature—and their Siamese heritage—means that they are a talkative or vocal breed. However, their voices are much softer and more melodic than the Siamese. They like to have 'conversations' with their owner.

The Snowshoe is also a very intelligent, agile, and active cat. It is really easy to train, loves playing games, and is very fond of high vantage points from which it can watch the world go by.

2) The Snowshoe's appearance

There are essentially three distinguishing marks for this beautiful breed: the white feet (the snow shoes), the inverted white "V" on the face, and the pointed coat.

The Snowshoe colouring varies greatly as the coat comes in a number of the typical Siamese colours. The breed also comes in two patterns but each Snowshoe has a pattern that is unique to that cat.

All purebred Snowshoes have blue eyes. The ears of these cats are medium sized and, unlike many other breeds, have slightly rounded tips rather than points. The eyes are larger than those of the Siamese and are walnut-shaped. The body is medium sized and muscular but never either chunky or delicate.

3) *Snowshoe Breeding Standards*

While different cat associations accept different patterns and colorations, the basic standards for the breed are:

- Head: triangular or apple-shaped
- Ears: medium to medium- large; slightly rounded tips
- Eyes: in purebreds the eyes must be blue; walnut shaped
- Body: medium sized; muscular and athletic; not dainty or chunky
- Coat: medium to short; no noticeable undercoat; bright and smooth; no double or plush coat
- Markings: points (ears, tail, face-mask, and sometimes legs) are solid black-based colours; variable white patterns, typically falling along the face, chest, stomach, and paws; even body coloration with subtle shading to point colour on back, shoulders and hips; toning to a lighter shade near the stomach and the chest
- Tail: medium sized, coming to a point
- Feet: medium in size and tapering to the toes; pads may be white, point colour, mottled, flesh tone, or chocolate brown in adults.

All of the associations and registries agree that the Snowshoe colour is the point coloration. In addition, the body colour should be lighter than the darker colours of the tail, face, ears, and legs. There are variations, however. The American Cat Fanciers Association and American Association of Cat Enthusiasts recognize both seal and blue point coloration. The Fédération Internationale Féline, on the other hand, recognizes seal, cream, fawn, blue, black, red, chocolate, and cinnamon coloration and tabby, tortoiseshell, and tortoiseshell-tabby patterning. The International Cat Association accepts all of the pointed colours.

Because the various cat associations are aware of the genetic challenges that the breed presents, they recognize and accept that no cat will have perfect markings. The cats at shows, therefore, that come closest to the ideal—an inverted white "V" between the eyes and over the muzzle, four solid white feet with dark points separating the white foot colour from the light body colour, and reasonably symmetrical markings—are the ones that win the rosettes.

4) Life span

The life expectancy for a Snowshoe is about the same as for any other breed of domestic cats. Snowshoes have been known to live for as many as 19 or 20 years. If you take good care of your cat you should be able to enjoy its company for at least 14-15 years.

5) Intelligence

The Snowshoe is acknowledged to be one of the most intelligent of the cat breeds with a healthy dose of natural feline curiosity. This means that they are both very easy to train and that they need regular stimulation and interaction from their owner or from another cat. The Snowshoe practically house trains itself. These cats can be taught to play fetch, sit, to walk on a lead or leash, use a toilet and even respond to some voice commands.

Because they are curious and intelligent these cats need mental stimulation. You can keep your cat mentally active by giving it puzzles and toys or by doing agility training with it. You will be surprised by how eager your cat will be to solve puzzles and go through an agility course.

Another quality that you will notice is that they will acquire skills like opening the door and even getting their toys out when they want them. Unfortunately they are not usually satisfied with just one toy. They need a several toys to stimulate their minds.

6) *How often to play with your Snowshoe*

If you pose this question to your Snowshoe it will reply, "All the time I'm awake and not eating or washing". That's a tall order and no cat owner cat live up to it. The solution for when you are not there or busy is to provide these energetic, sociable and acrobatic cats with a playmate—feline or canine—and a selection of fun toys. Your cat will find the toy it feels like playing with.

When you play with your cat, it will appear to go out of its way to make play time fun for you too because, for your cat, there's not much that's better than a fun, energetic game with you. The Snowshoe that gets attention and playtime will be a very happy, loving and relaxed cat.

7) *The amount of space they need*

These sociable, relaxed, medium size cats don't need much space. In addition, they are preferably indoor cats. This makes the Snowshoe the ideal cat to have, regardless of whether you live in an apartment or a house and do or don't have an outside area or a garden. As long as there is enough space for them to play, jump and run around they will be fit and contented. Because of their levels of energy and playfulness it takes very little encouragement from you, the owner to get exercise. Games that involve chasing an object such as a ball or a piece of string being pulled along to floor will give your cat loads of healthy exercise and be a huge amount of fun for you both. If you have more than one cat they will play games together.

8) *Indoor versus outdoor cats*

Contrary to popular belief it isn't cruel to keep a cat indoors. In addition, a breed like the Snowshoe where your cat is focused on you rather than the space it inhabits will be happy and content to be inside and with you. There are many reasons why keeping a cat indoors is preferable.

Outdoor cats, especially those that roam, are at much greater risk of picking up infections from the other cats. Not all cats your cat will come in contact with outside will be vaccinated or healthy. No cat owner wants to exposure their cat to the danger of possibly contracting a fatal illness such as Feline Leukaemia or Feline Immunodeficiency Virus both of which are easily transmitted and fairly common in cats that roam outside.

In addition to the risk of infection is the danger of injuries as a result of fights with other cats including strays or even feral cats. Some bites can lead to abscesses which can make a cat really sick very fast. Other illnesses such as rabies can be passed on by a bite or scratch from an infected cat.

Other cats are not the only animals that pose a potential threat to your Snowshoe. Domesticated cats that wander from their home are usually not able to defend themselves against animals like dogs, opossums, foxes and snakes. These encounters will often either result in serious injuries or even death immediately or some time later as a result of infection. If your cat wanders into the wrong areas it becomes vulnerable to attacks from any of these creatures that are either defending a territory or acting from fear or aggression. The other potentially dangerous creatures out there are people who have been known to poison, shoot or otherwise injure or kill cats.

Cats that roam around outside are also inevitably going to encounter a further danger: roads and traffic. Although many cats are smart enough to avoid the sound of approaching vehicles, a cat might run across a road if frightened by something such as a dog or a loud noise. In most cases an encounter with a car will result in very serious injury or death on impact.

Threats to your cat also come in the form of parasites such as fleas and ticks and fungi such as ringworm. Undergrowth, sand and stray or untreated cats harbour ticks and fleas are also a risk. Both of these insects could potentially get onto your Snowshoe. Fleas carry diseases that can potentially make your cat and you unwell.

Ticks are even more dangerous as certain types can paralyze or even kill a cat if not treated correctly. Tick bites for humans can cause serious illness too. A cat that wanders around outdoors could also pick up ringworm, which is easily transmitted to people. This is not a serious or life threatening problem but it is not easy to treat and tends to recur as a result.

A further danger facing an outdoor cat is getting lost. Cats can get distracted by an interesting scent, chase after a small animal or another cat and then lose its bearings. It is best not to dwell on the possibility that your Snowshoe could get stolen but it could happen. Even individuals who don't realise the value of a cat may take it because they like it, think it's a stray or to use for appalling things like religious practices or even to sell to a laboratory that does testing on animals. While the chance of these horrors is small, why take the risk?

Keeping a cat indoors avoids the potential for disputes with neighbours and ill-feeling. A cat might decide that a flower bed next door makes the ideal outdoor litter box. While performing the necessary excavations, plants might be uprooted or damaged. Even if there's no damage your neighbour is unlikely to be charmed with the new type of manure being deposited in her or his garden by your cat! There's also the possibility that your cat could get into a fight with a neighbourhood cat and you might be expected to pay the resulting vet bills. Finally, your male cat might not be popular if he impregnates the cat next door.

Keep in mind that the most important thing in your cat's life will be you. This means that your Snowshoe cat, whether male or female, will be more than happy to be a home-body if you are there and if he or she has some company, or at least a few toys, and enough food and water when you are out. Given they are very intelligent and curious these cats are unlikely to get bored and playing with them will give them enough exercise and stimulation to keep them fit physically and emotionally.

Given all of these factors in favour of keeping your cat inside it is hardly surprising to learn that indoor cats have much healthier and longer lives that their outdoor counterparts. If you are reluctant, however, to keep your cat inside but don't want your Snowshoe to roam there is the option of building a cat enclosure. A cat enclosure is much more than a cage. Regardless of the amount of space you have available outside, you can create of really fun and safe outdoor area for your Snowshoe. It will of course have to be enclosed and you need to use cat proof fences. The height of a fence is a consideration too as a cat can leap five times its own height from a standing position.

You could either build an enclosure yourself or purchase one. If you have a significant amount of space – and a fair bit of money – available, a cat enclosure can be large enough to include ramps, sleeping platforms, tunnels for play, tree branches and so on. Remember to provide both warm and shaded spots. An alternative, if you have less space, is a cat run. This could be an enclosed narrow strip down the side of a house or an enclosed veranda or balcony. With a smaller space such as a balcony you could use cat netting. Again, the addition of things to climb up, onto or through will make it a fun, stimulating place for your cat.

Regardless of whether you have an enclosure or run for your Snowshoe, you must make sure that it has easy and safe access to it through a window or cat flap. If the enclosure is some distance from the house, you could consider an enclosed tunnel from the point of exit from your home to the enclosure. This way your cat has exercise just getting to and from its outdoor enclosure!

9) The Snowshoe anatomy

Average adult size and weight

The Snowshoe is a medium sized, well proportioned cat that is neither too big nor too small. These cats look like runners and jumpers thanks to their trim, muscular builds and they are indeed powerful and agile.

Average weight for an adult male is 9 to 12 pounds (4.8 – 5.5 kilograms). The smaller female usually weighs in at between 7 and 10 pounds (3 – 4.5 kilograms); however, some females weigh as much as the males without seeming as solid.

Pigmentation and colours

The Snowshoe colouring varies greatly as the coat comes in seal, blue, red, cream, chocolate, fawn, lilac, and cinnamon, which are the typical Siamese colours. The most common are seal point and blue point. The breed comes in two patterns: bicolour and mitted (white).

Interestingly, all Snowshoe kittens are born white with point colour developing as they grow and mature over the first three weeks of their lives. The head, ears, legs and tail darken as the kitten gets older.

While purebreds have sparkling blue eyes, Snowshoe eye colours range from this gorgeous blue to a lovely pale blue-grey.

Chapter 4: Before you buy your Snowshoe

1) Questions to ask before bringing a Snowshoe home

The first issue you need to consider before buying a Snowshoe, or any other pet for that matter, is whether you are prepared and able to be a responsible owner. There are several lifestyle factors that a potential Snowshoe owner must consider:

1. **Time**: a Snowshoe kitten or cat will thrive on a great deal of play time. If your work or social life takes you away from home a great deal this could be a problem because these cats are not good at being left alone.

2. **Environment**: is your living space sufficiently large to accommodate an active cat? Are there things in your environment which pose a danger to an animal? If there are any hazards in the environment, are you able to easily remove these?

3. **Cost**: the first significant cost is the price you will have to pay for the Snowshoe kitten or cat that you choose. Thereafter they will be regular expenses including food, vet or medical expenses, grooming products and other incidentals such as bedding, toys, scratching post et cetera.

4. **Patience**: litter box training is fairly quick but there may be a few accidents at first. Also, as with any boisterous animal your kitten may knock over and break items.

2) The shopping list for your new kitten or cat

There are several items that should, preferably, be acquired before you fetch your Snowshoe and bring your new companion home.

Food and related items

The first item is food. Obviously the type of food you purchase will depend of whether you are going to bring a kitten or a cat home; different aged cats have differing nutritional needs. It is recommended that you purchase a mixture of canned food and dry food. Like people, cats enjoy a varied diet. On the can or the bag of food it will clearly state the age of the cat that the food has been formulated for.

Some Snowshoe owners are great supporters of a diet of bones and raw food for their cats. However, this is not recommended with very young cats.

In addition to the food itself, you will need to purchase food and water bowls. It's always a good idea to have more than one per cat so that you can insure that you have a clean bowl to use at all times. As you are not going to be with your cat all the time, it can be a very good idea to purchase an automatic food dispenser. This way your cat will not be without food at any stage during the day or night.

Cat Litter

There is a vast array of cat litters available commercially. The general rule of thumb is to avoid scented litters; while you might prefer them it's highly unlikely that your cat with its highly developed sense of smell will. Cat litters that clump are also to be avoided, especially if you have a young cat that might eat some of the litter and subsequently suffer from blockages in the digestive system.

Working out what the best litter is for your cat is a question of trial and error. Eventually you will find the one that your cat responds to best and that you don't find to onerous to clean or replace. If you ever run out of clean cat litter an emergency measure that works very effectively is either soil or sand from your garden or shredded newspaper.

Bed and bedding

While it's not always necessary to buy a bed and bedding for a cat it can be a good idea. Of course, given you are dealing with a cat you could buy a bed that will be ignored in favour of a couch, a chair or your bed!

Toys

There is also a wide range of toys available for cats and kittens that vary in sophistication and cost. You could certainly choose one or two of these to have at your home for when your new charge arrives.

Alternatively, it is not always necessary to buy toys as one can make them. For example, a kitten or cat will have hours of enjoyment chasing the end of a piece of string, jumping up to catch a cork or a small ball suspended by piece of string. It is perhaps better to get to know your cat a little before deciding what sort of toys he or she is likely to respond to best.

Scratching post

It's not only important for your cat to have a scratching post to keep their claws sharp, you and your furniture need this piece of equipment too because your cat is far less likely to sharpen its claws on your furniture. A scratching post is necessary to help keep your cat's claws healthy too. And it's another item for your Snowshoe to play with…

Clothing

Opinion is divided about clothing for cats in general. Many cat owners believe that clothing is unnatural on a cat and it just causes the animal stress and, in the worst case scenario, an adverse skin reaction.

3) Removing household hazards

Medicine

One of the most toxic substances for a cat is your prescription medications or drugs. They are in fact the most common cause of poisoning in cats. For instance, an ingredient like ibuprofen, which is found in many painkillers, is deadly for cats.

Just as you would for children, you must ensure that all drugs or medications are kept where your cat cannot find them and ingest them.

Electrical appliances

While it's not always possible to remove electrical appliances or their cords, one needs to take care with them because kittens and young cats like playing with moving or dangling objects. An electrical cord attached to an iron, for example, will be irresistible to a young kitten. Your cat will pull on the cord or swing from it.

This could be very dangerous for both the cat and your property. In addition, if the cat's teeth penetrate the cord's plastic covering he or she will receive an electric shock.

Poisons

Cats are foragers by nature. Snowshoe cats are especially curious and adventurous. It is therefore very important that you don't leave any garden pest powders, pellets and sprays; weed killers; cleaning materials; contaminated foods or foods toxic to cats exposed and accessible. If you do, your cat will find them and, although they are not indiscriminate eaters, there is a chance that poison could be ingested.

Poisonous plants

There are certain plants you may have in a garden or indoors or potted plants that are poisonous or potentially deadly for cats. In fact, the list of plants toxic to cats is astonishingly lengthy. It includes Rhododendrons and Azaleas, Lily-of-the-Valley, the lily family, Amaryllis, Holly, Asparagus Fern, Begonia, Clivia, Chrysanthemums and Cycads to name just a few. A general rule of thumb is that plants with variegated leaves should be avoided as they are more toxic than others.

It is possible that your Snowshoe will decide to snack on a pot plant, especially if it is an indoor cat. You will have to decide how great a risk the plants you have pose.

Swimming pools

If you have a swimming pool a secure pool cover is a good idea while your cat is young. Don't ever leave a kitten near a pool or even a pond unattended. If your neighbour has a pool or pond there's not much you can do about it.

However, once your cat is settled, you can and should teach it about pool safety (see the relevant section of "Training" in chapter 6). This should not be hard as the Snowshoe is one of the few breeds that actually enjoys water and will swim!

Doors and windows

When you bring your new kitten, or more especially your new cat, home for the first time, you must see that all the windows and external doors are closed. The Snowshoe is a stay-at-home cat by nature, but any cat that is confronted by new sights, sounds, smells and people may panic and dash about initially. The last thing you want is for a frightened cat to vanish through an open door and window!

Heat sources

Some sources of heat are dangerous for a cat to be around. You need to take precautions to prevent your cat being burnt. You need to be careful with stoves, stove hot plates, heaters, exposed light bulbs, fireplaces and the inside of large appliances that may be warm. Your cat may cosy up to any one of these and not realize till it's too late that its delicate skin has been affected. Try to screen open or accessible heat sources within the home and close appliances such as tumble dryers so your cat can't climb in.

Chapter 5: Choosing your Snowshoe

Choosing the Snowshoe that is going to become your companion is both important and difficult. This is especially the case if you are confronted by a number of kittens, each with its own personality and characteristics. Selecting a kitten using the, "Ooh! That one is *so* cute!" method is not good enough. You must take your time to find the kitten that is right for you.

While much of your decision will be based on the kitten or cat itself, if you are getting a kitten from a breeder then he or she will also impact on your choice. If the breeder has socialized the kittens they will be happy – or at least comfortable – to be picked up and handled. If the kittens aren't and seem fearful of people or nervous this is an indication that they have not been well treated and may exhibit behavioural problems now and / or later in life.

You also need to assess the kitten or cat's state of health. Have a careful look at the eyes, which should be clear and bright. Make sure that there is no discharge from its eyes, ears or nose. The gums and tongue should be pink. Watch that the kitten's gait is even. Ensure that the kitten has good hearing and eyesight by making a noise and moving your finger. If the kitten turns to the sound and follows the movement it means their sight and hearing are fine.

After you have looked at health and general behaviour you can sit back and watch the kittens play and interact, look at markings and eye colour if that is important to you, and consider things such as personality, energy levels and curiosity.

It is worth taking your time to choose the kitten that will be right for you. The wrong choice may result in having to return the kitten which will be upsetting for you and traumatic for the kitten.

1) General considerations

Getting one or two cats

As stated previously, Snowshoe cats are extremely sociable and loving. They adore company and need affection. If you are away from home each day, to go to work for example, then it is a good idea to get two cats.

They will be play companions and can curl up and sleep together in your absence. They will also provide moral support to each other when they confront a new situation.

Buying a male or female

This is a hotly debated question and it can be an important consideration. Some believe that male and female cats are cast in similar stereotypical moulds as their human counterparts: males are more physical, even aggressive, and females are gentler.

However, other cat owners – me included – have had experiences that prove the opposite: gentle, stay-at-home (neutered) males and females prone to bouts of ill temper and sulking. Many believe that one should choose a kitten or cat based on health and personality; don't let gender be the deciding factor.

The age a kitten should be when you buy it

A reputable breeder won't allow anyone to take a kitten that is younger than 12 weeks old. They need to be weaned correctly, have time to get strong and be socialised and to have the required vaccinations and deworming.

A registered versus a non-registered kitten

If you obtain a kitten from a registered and reputable breeder, a registered kitten comes with a number of advantages.

Firstly, you know that your Snowshoe kitten is actually a purebred Snowshoe. Secondly, you can rest assured that the kitten is old enough to leave its mother and it has been socialized. In addition, a registered cat is far less likely to carry genetic or other illnesses. A professional breeder will also have had the necessary vaccinations done and the kitten will be dewormed.

With an unregistered kitten you have none of these assurances; there's no guarantee the kitten is either healthy or even a Snowshoe.

2) What to ask the breeder

When you talk to breeders, either when you are selecting one or before choosing your Snowshoe, there are a number of issues you need to discuss and investigate.

The breeder and the facility

To begin with, you want to know about the breeder and the facility. You need to ask to see proof of his or her registration as a Snowshoe breeder.

A tour of the breeder's premises is also recommended. Where are the cats housed? Are the rooms, runs or areas the cats are in clean, airy and spacious? If a breeder refuses to let you look around, leave!

The kitten or cat's lineage and the breeding pair

You should ask the breeder about the kitten's lineage, including the age of the mother and father because cats should not be bred past the age of 4 or 5.

You also want assurances, and preferably proof, of the health of the breeding pair in terms of vaccinations and overall health. If you intend to show your cat you should also establish if the parents have ever been shown as this indicates breed standard.

Meeting the breeding pair will also help you to get an idea of the size their offspring will reach and also give you an indication of personality as the mother in particular influences this.

Medical documentation

Finally, request proof from the breeder that the kitten has had its vaccinations, been dewormed and declared fit by a vet. The breeder must also provide you with a health guarantee. If he or she refuses, be suspicious.

The kitten's temperament

This, too, will be hinted at by the temperament and nature of the kitten's mother. However, the breeder will have – or should have – spent a lot of time with the kittens. Ask him or her about the temperament and personality of the kittens on offer or of the one that you are interested in.

Of course, your own observations while you watch the kittens play and when you interact will also tell you a lot about them. It is not hard to see which kittens are shy, extroverted, adventurous, playful and so on. You know what you are looking for in your Snowshoe companion so watch for those qualities.

Chapter 6: Your new Snowshoe kitten or cat

1) The first important few hours

When you get to your home with your new Snowshoe, it is recommended that you restrict him or her to just one or two rooms initially. Firstly, too much too soon can be overwhelming for a kitten or even an adult cat whose sense of hearing and smell is far more acute than ours. Secondly, housetraining is a little easier for you if your kitten is not allowed to go everywhere at the beginning. Finally, it allows you to bond with your cat and have control over how and when your Snowshoe meets the other members of the household.

Don't be concerned or offended if your new kitten or cat's first act when you get home is to go into hiding. It might choose to crawl back into the carrier it arrived in or find another spot. It's not a bad idea to provide a few hiding spots that are easy to get into and out of. When your new Snowshoe is ready it will emerge and begin to cautiously explore the new room it finds itself in. Don't force the issue; wait till he or she is ready to come out of hiding.

It can be a good idea to close the new arrival into this room and leave it on its own for an hour or so to give it a chance to calm down. Make sure that you have placed food and water in the room along with bedding and a cat litter box. Keep in mind that cats are clean creatures so don't place the cat box near the food and water bowls. Leaving a few toys in the room will also help your new companion begin to relax.

You must never reach for the cat or try to cuddle in the beginning. If your cat is not nervous by nature, it may just come to you on its own. What you should do, however, is visit the cat regularly. Walk into the bonding room, sit on the floor or a low seated chair for a while and call out to him in a voice that is soothing. It is okay for you to walk in and out of the room as long as you leave your kitten or cat alone for a couple of hours in between. Even if it takes several sessions to get your cat to even greet you, don't lose your patience.

In case there are children in your family, make sure that they visit the cat only when they are accompanied by an adult. At least in the initial days, this is mandatory. The reason to take this precaution is that children might get excited at the sight of the cat. If they startle the cat, he might just become anxious and even scratch or harm the child. So, never let children near the cat without proper supervision.

2) Settling in

Bringing you new Snowshoe home for the fist time is both exciting and a little scary. It should be the start of a wonderful, long relationship so one must begin well. Keep in mind that there is a great deal that is new for the kitten or cat to adjust to; don't try and do it all at once.

If you work, try to collect your kitten or cat at a time, like a Saturday morning, so that you can spend the whole weekend with him or her to make the transition easier and so you can bond. The time you take to bond with your new Snowshoe is an important investment in your relationship that will stand you both in good stead for many years to come. You need to take the time and make an effort to get to know each other.

As I mentioned, cats have very acute hearing and smell. Your home is going to present your new Snowshoe with a host of sounds and smells that are new and sometimes intimidating. Things that are ordinary to us will sound very loud and scary to a newly arrived kitten or cat. To help him or her with this, there are a few guidelines to follow.

When you talk to your new kitten do so softly and don't pick it up too often. The sound and smell of you is new, too. Also, don't play music or the TV very loud. Wait to use the vacuum cleaner until your Snowshoe has bonded with you and started to settle in. At the very least, don't vacuum the room your kitten or cat is placed in when it first arrives so that it has a non-threatening space to be in. Hosting parties or dinner parties and having a line of people trooping in and out to admire or meet your new cat is also not a good idea.

3) Bringing home an adult Snowshoe

An adult cat needs to be treated differently to a kitten. You need to take a few additional steps before bringing an adult Snowshoe home.

First, an adult cat will usually take a little longer to settle than a kitten. Why? Because adult cats, like adult people, have a history and past experiences that result in established patterns of behaviour along with likes and dislikes. If you can find out what these are it will help you and your new Snowshoe. If you get your cat from a breeder you can find about its past and interactions with people and other animals. If your new cat comes from a shelter you may not be able to get any information and will have to be guided by your cat's reactions.

31

You can also ask about food, toy and activity likes and dislikes. Being able to provide things you know your new companion is familiar with and enjoys will help him or her settle more easily. You could also enquire about things that the cat finds frightening. For instance, I once acquired a cat who was affectionate, laid-back, funny and usually fairly fearless. However, he was terrified of plastic grocery bags! At the sound or sight of one he would run. Somewhere in his past something unpleasant with a plastic bag had happened. I made a point never to have one anywhere near him.

Adult cats, if necessary, can be kept in a cat carrier for a few days. The carrier should be placed in the room that the cat will be confined to once it leaves the carrier. In fact, the carrier can be left in an out-of-the-way place permanently for use by your cat when it feels frightened, anxious or under the weather.

Just as with a kitten, there must always be food – preferably one the cat is familiar with and likes – and fresh water available. A litter box is also necessary. When kittens and cats are accustomed to the sound and scent of their new owner it's important to spend as much time as possible with it as part of the settling in phase.

Once there is less likelihood of accidents, and your new Snowshoe has left the room it was initially confined to, it's a very good idea to keep your kitten or cat company as it explores the entire home. Only when it has examined everything and every room will it decide which spots will be its resting, sleeping and hiding places.

Your new adult Snowshoe needs to be watched. If your cat is not eating or using the litter box, showing signs of restlessness, being very vocal or scratching or licking excessively you may need to consult a vet as these are possible signs of stress and unhappiness.

4) Preparing your family for a pet

It is not only you and your home that must be ready for your new arrival. Everyone in the house must be prepared. Young children especially are usually so delighted to see a pet that they might shout, rush at or attempt to pick it up. This would not be what your Snowshoe needs!

All the occupants of your home need to be informed about the cat that will be joining the household: when it will arrive, what it will look like, the changes that must be made both during the settling in phase and afterwards, to be patient and give the cat time and space to adjust and not to expect or try to handle or play with it immediately. With the Snowshoe the waiting period before it is ready to have social and fun time with the family shouldn't be too long as they are so playful and gregarious by nature.

You will also need to make sure everybody knows about feeding, the litter box requirements, not feeding the cat unhealthy treats, keeping medicines and other poisons safely put away and keeping doors and windows closed until the initial period is safely negotiated.

Also, given cats love to explore and will sometimes go to sleep in odd places, the family must get into the habit of checking inside big appliances such as washing machines, tumble dryers and dishwashers before turning them on.

5) Make time for your new cat

One can't say this often enough: the Snowshoe cat loves and needs attention! It's not necessary to play with it, as until it is feeling relaxed and settled it is unlikely to feel like playing, but you must spend time in the same room with it and speak to it in a friendly and soothing tone.

Just sit in the room and give your new companion time to get used to your scent and the way you sound, look and move. Family members can take turns spending time with the new arrival but at the beginning it should just be you.

Playtime

This can start in earnest with your new cat once it is used to the new surroundings. How can you tell? Your Snowshoe will emerge from hiding and want to include you in his or her territory. You will know you have been accepted and marked when your new companion rubs its head, body or face on you to leave their scent. You are now their person!

Even if your new cat now rubs itself against your legs it may still resist overtures from you. If you reach out to stroke or touch the cat or kitten and it backs off you can either leave it and give it a little more time or your could lure it with toys… A shoe lace or piece of string pulled along the ground is pretty irresistible to the majority of cats who will immediately give chase and pounce. A high energy and interactive game like this is the ideal ice breaker between you and your new Snowshoe.

6) Complicated scenarios

You will have to do a little extra work if you are introducing your new Snowshoe into a household in which there is a child, a dog or another cat or cats. This is because if there are other animals there are hierarchies and pecking orders already in place that your new arrival will have to fit into. However, there are steps one can take that will make the transition much smoother for all concerned.

Introducing your Snowshoe to your dog

Another of the many advantages of this breed is that they get on well with dogs. That is assuming of course that the dog is cat-friendly. No breed will be comfortable with a dog that thinks cats are for chasing or make great snacks! If you are not quite sure how your dog will behave there are a few things you can do to make sure that there are no problems.

While your new Snowshoe is in the bonding room for the post-arrival period don't let the dog in. What does help is to get them used to each other's scents or pheromones before they meet in person. An easy way to achieve this is by feeding them on either side of the door. Of course if your dog starts barking or scratching at the door you must move him or her further away and then move the bowl closer to the door again gradually. Eventually they will become familiar with each other's smell. It's time to move on to the next step once they can both quietly get on with their meals with just the door between them.

When the first face-to-face introduction takes place, it is wise to put a leash on both the dog and the Snowshoe. In all probability your cat will be interested and fairly relaxed. Once you are sure that your dog is not going to give chase and isn't showing any signs of aggression, take the leash off the cat. It will help considerably if your dog is trained with basic commands such as, "Sit" and "Stay". If not, consider doing so. You can also use treats to reward your dog each time it interacts positively with your cat.

Even though the Snowshoe does interact well with dogs and many times will play with and even sleep curled up with a dog, keep in mind that dogs and cats can be unpredictable. Until you are 100% sure that there is harmony between them, especially if your Snowshoe is still a kitten, don't leave them alone together. Even a playful bite from a dog could badly injure or even kill a kitten or a cat if the dog is large and really attacking.

If your dog is just not accepting your new cat and continues to bark and or snap at it you may have to get professional advice about how you can modify the behaviour and get your dog to calm down. Alternatively, you may have to return the cat…

Introducing your Snowshoe to an existing cat or cats

If there is already a resident cat in your home, expect your new Snowshoe to become more dominant with familiarity. It is stressful to your old pet to deal with the fact that there is another cat in the house. Quite obviously, it is stressful for you as well to make sure that your older cat does not feel neglected or out of place. You need to follow a process to make the situation more relaxed for you, your older cat and your new Snowshoe.

The first direct interaction should preferably be scheduled over a weekend so that you have all day to spend with the new cat and your cat-in-residence. This way, you can make sure that there are no unpleasant incidents and so that you can intervene if needs be.

It is usually best to get your older cat and new Snowshoe to interact during a meal time. Some growling and hissing, especially initially, is to be expected as both will want to assert themselves to some degree. However, it will not be entirely aggressive. To make sure that it does not get out of hand, though, you must place their feeding bowls at opposite ends of the room and you must stay with them. Once the feeding is done, separate them again.

Most cats are territorial by nature although your Snowshoe's main territory will be you. Make sure you establish the boundaries for both the cats. When your new cat is out of the confinement from its bonding or settling in room, you might want to make a special corner for him or her that is not too close to the existing space of you resident cat. Just place the feeding bowl and the cat bed in the designated area with your cat's favourite toys.

The interactions between your cats must be gradual so they become used to each other and neither feels threatened or rushed. You can try the blanket switching technique with cats so that they become more used to each other's scents or pheromones. When they are accustomed to each others' scent, they will become comfortable with each other. Increase the time they spend with each other slowly. Only when you are quite certain that they are relaxed in each other's company can you leave them alone and unsupervised. Until then you must never leave them unattended in the same space. This is especially true for night times when cats are naturally at their most active.

If you already have more than one cat at home, you will notice that one of the resident cats will take the initiative to introduce the new cat to the existing group. If this happens you are in luck as they will probably handle the situation far better than you could!

It is not uncommon for cats to not get along immediately although the Snowshoe gets on better with other cats far better than most other breeds. But, if your resident cat and the new kitten or cat doesn't hit it off make sure you do not punish either of them. You just need to separate them when they get anxious. You must understand that this behaviour is purely instinctive. With regular interactions, the cats will learn to live together peacefully and will decide who is who in terms of seniority or pecking order.

Your new Snowshoe and babies or toddlers

As a rule, Snowshoe cats are tolerant of children and gentle with them. However, it is quite possible – and perfectly natural – that young children will get excited around a kitten or a cat. This excitement usually manifests itself as excited shouts or squeals when they first catch sight of the new kitty.

In addition to these noises, which will be very loud and alarming for a new cat, a child also looks, behaves and smells very different from an adult. This unfamiliarity is not only distressing for the cat but also potentially dangerous for a child. There are some rules to introducing your child to the new cat that will reduce the trauma and possibility of injuries to either the cat or the child.

Make sure that your new cat and your child or children have regular interactions as soon as your new Snowshoe has started to settle and is comfortable around you. At no point should you allow the child to venture alone into the room where the new cat is still settling. You can teach your child to call and talk to the cat soothingly and even just watch the cat quietly until it gets accustomed to the child or children's presence.

It's also important to teach children not to run at or grab at a cat, as that will alarm the cat greatly as it won't understand this is a gesture of enthusiasm and affection! Children also need to be told that the cat is not a toy. You must constantly remind your child to be gentle. An enthusiastic, loving and well-intentioned hug from a toddler can result in injuries in a kitten or cat or just frighten it badly. A child needs to be taught how to hold, pick up and handle a kitten or cat and learn that pulling an ear or tail can be really painful for the cat. Also, a cat or kitten that is hurt or angry may instinctively retaliate and cause a child some pain from a scratch or a nip. If this happens, comfort your child but don't punish the cat.

Scent from hormones called pheromones are very important in the animal world. In fact, many animals relate to things purely on the basis of their smell. Cats use other senses too but scent shouldn't be underestimated. It is therefore a good idea to let your child handle some of the cat's items such as bedding or toys so that their scent is left behind for the cat to get used to. If he or she is old enough you can give your child a responsibility like handling the cat's blanket or just filling up the food or water bowl.

With much younger children like toddlers it is not realistic to give him or her responsibility for caring for the cat, but you could use the sock technique to introduce them to each other. Rub one of your toddler's socks on the cat's cheek. Then, let the toddler wear the sock. Because of this rubbing off of the scent, the cat will smell its own scent on the sock and view the toddler as a friend that he or she can trust.

Snowshoe cat owners all stress how tolerant and adaptable their cats are. They are very gentle and loving cats and will therefore usually make truly great companions for children to play with. In fact, children and Snowshoe cats often develop very close bonds.

Over and above the time you must spend getting your cat settled, introduced to the other residents, cuddling and playing with your new kitten or cat, you need to start training… for both your sakes!

7) *Training*

While the Snowshoe is an extremely intelligent cat it is still a cat. This means that your kitten will be as good at training you as you are at training it. The ease with which you train a cat increases in direct proportion to the degree to which they want to be trained. In your favour, in addition to their intelligence, is the Snowshoe cat's desire to please.

Scratch Training

Getting a cat to use a scratching post rather than your furniture is usually fairly easy. Cats naturally look for a rough surface to sharpen their claws. They need to do this. You should incorporate the scratching post into play sessions in the first few days. Scratch the surface of the post with your finger nail or nails. The sound alone will get your kitten interested. As soon as he or she tries to catch your finger they will be introduced to a surface they like the feel of.

Continue to do this for a few days and your smart Snowshoe should go on using the post and leave your sofa and table legs alone. You can also use a Catnip spray on the surface of the scratching post as an added attraction. These sprays are available from pet shops and vets. Just remember to reapply the spray every three or four days as the scent fades.

Another option – if you have a cat that keeps scratching a piece of furniture such as a sofa – is to use broad packaging tape along the sections of the fabric furnishings that your cat is energetically targeting. Cats do not like either the feel or smell of the tape and this very quickly breaks them of the habit.

Litter Box Training

This is an important area of training, as nobody wants a cat that is not housetrained. In this regard you will be assisted by the intelligence of the Snowshoe and the inherently fastidious and clean feline nature.

Keep in mind that a kitten is a baby. Like human babies it will be busy playing or doing something and not realize till the last minute that it needs to urinate or defecate. For this reason, you need to expect the odd accident and be sensible about where you place the litter box. Your kitten will sometimes need to get to it in a hurry.

The best places to put a litter box are away from areas where the cat eats, where food is stored or prepared and in a quite place (cats like privacy too). A corner is also usually ideal. If your house is large or has more than one level, it can be a good idea to have more than one litter box. Also, if you have more than one cat, you will need more than one box because cats don't like to share. Finally, don't move the litter box around so that your kitten or cat knows where to find it.

It is very important to show your kitten where the litter box is. One needs to establish a routine:

- ✓ Place your kitten gently into the litter box a few minutes after a meal and after he or she wakes up
- ✓ Be patient. Give your kitten time to walk around and sniff the litter box
- ✓ The instinct to dig and bury waste usually emerges on its own. If it doesn't, gently take a front paw and show him or her how to dig and scratch in the sand. Alternatively, dig a little hole in the (clean) litter with your fingers
- ✓ Every time your Snowshoe kitten uses the litter box give it lots of praise and cuddles
- ✓ Don't ever shout at or otherwise frighten a kitten in a litter box because he or she will make a negative association.

40

Furthermore, if you are spending time with your kitten and watching it you will notice the signs that it needs to use the box. Don't rush at or alarm it; gently pick it up and place it in the litter tray.

Once the litter box has been used the likelihood that the kitten will return increases as his or her scent has been left behind. In the event of an accident – and these will happen – you can take some of the waste and place it in the box as this might help to increase the scent levels and strengthen the association.

And don't ever shout at or hit a kitten that has had an accident. It won't know what you are angry about and will begin to fear you or feel nervous instead of understanding why you are upset or angry. It is far better if you praise good behaviour – the use of the litter box – and intervene when you see an accident is imminent in order to re-enforce the connection.

In order to encourage your kitten to make the transition from litter box to outdoor area or garden, you just need to slowly move the litter box closer and closer to the external door that the kitten or the cat will use. Eventually you will move the litter box to just outside the door. When you see your kitten or cat in the litter box and about to use it, pick it up gently and show it a suitable patch of earth that is soft enough to dig in. In time he or she will pick their favourite spots.

Toilet Training

Most of us are happy to teach our kittens and cats to use a litter box and then, if we can, gradually teach them to use the garden or an outside area. There are, however, some patient cat owners who want their cat to use the toilet. The nature and temperament of the Snowshoe certainly will help with this more complex training, especially if you disguise it as a game.

The first step is to place the litter box on the floor, right next to the toilet, for a few days. Thereafter you will need to gradually raise the litter box until it is at the same height as the toilet seat. At the same time as raising the box, you need to gradually decrease the amount of litter in it.

The next stage in the process involves moving the box onto the toilet seat in 1" (2.5cm) increments. Eventually the box will be directly over the seat and there should only be a very thin layer of litter left in it.

At this point the litter box is replaced with a training box. You have two options: a commercially available product or a homemade one. If you opt for the latter you can fasten wax paper, plastic or (aluminium) foil over the toilet bowl, under the seat. Sprinkle a handful of litter onto the training box.

A word of caution: make sure whatever material you use is strong enough to hold the weight of the kitten or cat when it steps onto it or jumps up. If he or she falls in the toilet that's it; you can forget toilet training!

The next stage is to cut a hole that is 1" (2.5cm) in diameter in the material you have used. Gradually increase the diameter until the material is almost cut back right to the bowl. At this stage of the training the sprinkling of litter has gone entirely.

Finally, remove the training box or seat entirely. Don't teach your Snowshoe to flush; they can enjoy it so much it will drive you nuts and waste a lot of water! You will have to flush the toilet yourself.

Water and bathing

This training is also far easier with a Snowshoe than with the majority of breeds because they actually enjoy playing with water and swimming! This is also very useful if you do decide to give your cat a bath.

Swimming pools

These cats might enjoy water and even go swimming but that doesn't mean they can't drown. It is very important that you show your cat where to get out of the water and give it enough practice in doing so that your Snowshoe will be able to get itself out of the water without difficulty even if you are not there to help.

Doing tricks

Some feel that cats shouldn't be trained to do tricks because it is somehow beneath their dignity. This is a very personal choice. Actually it will probably be your cat's decision rather than yours; some cats are just not interested. There is no doubt that the intelligence and eagerness to entertain and please found in the Snowshoe means that one can train them to do tricks far more easily than many breeds.

There are numerous instances of cats that play fetch and the Snowshoe is one breed that loves this game. As with any behaviour you want to reinforce and encourage, rewards are very important as motivators for your cat. With a Snowshoe the treat doesn't have to be edible because your cat will be addicted to affection and cuddles. So, stroking him or her or playing a fun game will also be an effective reward.

Some cats also sit on command. This can be achieved by holding a treat above the cat's head and saying, "Sit!" If he or she does, hand over the treat. If not, repeat the command while gently but firmly pushing the cat's bottom down and then giving a treat. Keep this routine up until the cat sits when asked to.

Agility training

Agility training is something you can do with your Snowshoe just because it is fun for both of you rather than because you want to enter or compete in agility shows or contests. It is also a wonderful way to exercise an indoor cat.

Your Snowshoe will be ideal for agility activities for several reasons. Firstly, these are intelligent cats that thrive on new activities, stimulation and challenges. Secondly, they are easy to train thanks to both their intelligence and enthusiasm. Finally, your cat will love playing and spending this one-on-one time with you.

You don't need special equipment for agility training. You can use things around the house to set up an agility course that provides things to jump or climb over and tunnels to run through. A paper bag cut open at both ends makes good a tunnel. A wooden, long handled utensil such as a spoon balanced on top of two mugs or rolls of toilet paper will make a perfectly good hurdle. Of course you can buy equipment from a supplier. Either way, remember that you must build an agility course that should be like a playground for your cat. Keep your cat's age and size in mind so you don't expect too much or push too hard. It must be fun for both of you.

You can start agility training when a kitten is really young. Just be patient and gentle and stop when your kitty shows signs of being tired or losing interest. Remember this is supposed to be fun, not military boot camp! Don't ever force your cat to do anything. If your cat seems tired or indicates it has had enough give your Snowshoe a rest and try again later or the next day. It is important, though, to do these agility activities with your cat every day.

Using a toy of some kind that will grab your kitten or cat's attention and lure it through a tunnel or hoop or over an obstacle is a very effective training tool. There are cat toys with feathers on them that are not too expensive and are ideal for this purpose. Wiggle the toy at the end of the tunnel or other side of an obstacle to entice your cat through or over it. A cat's natural desire to chase and pounce will work with you.

As with any training, treats should be used to reward the cat each time it does something correctly or well. You can also use a clicker bought from a vet store. Clicker training means that when your cat gets it right you 'click' and give it a treat. Do not forget the treat must be accompanied by verbal praise and cuddles.

8) How long a Snowshoe can be left alone

If you asked your Snowshoe this question the answer would be along the lines of, "Not at all… Please!" These affectionate and gregarious cats do not like being alone. If you need to go out for a few hours your cat will cope, but he or she won't be happy. If you will be away at work each day, all day, then you must get your cat a companion so that he or she does not become stressed, lonely and even depressed. You don't have to have a second Snowshoe; just so long as it is a friendly animal and the two of them get along well.

9) Transporting your Snowshoe

Much of this is really common sense… Never drive or travel in a car with a cat sitting on your lap or on the back or the front seat. The cat could very easily become frightened, jump onto the driver or get under the driver's feet and cause an accident. Use a carry cage or basket to contain the cat. Do not use a cardboard box, as the cat may escape or claw its way out if it is very frightened. If you must leave your cat in the car on a hot day, make sure that the car is parked in a cool, shaded spot and that the windows are down slightly to allow some airflow. Before leaving on a long journey, restrict the cat's food and water intake for 2 to 3 hours. In hot weather, the cat will need to have a drink now and then throughout the day.

10) To microchip your cat or not

The reason to micro-chip an animal is to help to trace it if it is lost. A microchip is one aspect of cat identification. The other is a break-away collar with a disc. Although a chip can be effective, it is not fool-proof. The down side is that having a chip will only help if someone takes your cat to a shelter if it gets lost. Also, while most animal shelters have scanners and use them, this is not true of all of them. This is why also having a collar and tag is a good idea.

The procedure is fairly simple and should, preferable, be done by a vet. A large needle is used to place the chip, which is about the size of a grain of rice, under the skin, between the cat's shoulder blades. A special scanner can read the unique number on the chip. The procedure only takes a few seconds and the sensation is the same as having blood drawn. In other words, there is a little pain and discomfort but it is very brief.

There is an extremely small possibility of complications happening after the chip implant. For instance, a few animals have developed tumours at the site where the chip was placed. This is, however, statistically very unlikely.

The cost of micro-chipping at time of writing is in the region of $50 in America and up to £40 in the UK depending on when it's done and who does it. If you are going to have this procedure done, you can take your cat in to the vet from the age of 12 weeks onwards.

The chips used in different parts of the world also utilize different frequencies. The UK and Europe use a 134.2 kilohertz chip while a 125 and 128 kilohertz chip is used in America. If you are going to take your cat across a border you should check in advance on the requirements as some countries have regulations about both chip date and type.

Chapter 7: Feeding your Snowshoe

1) What to feed your kitten and how often

A kitten's nutritional needs and digestive capabilities are not the same as those of an adult cat. For the first year of your cat's life you will need to give it a balanced diet using a good quality kitten food that you can purchase either from your vet or a pet shop. If you are unsure what brand to buy, ask your vet for advice.

If you decide you want to feed your little Snowshoe raw meat you must keep in mind that this diet won't provide all the nutrition and trace elements that a growing cat needs. As a result you will also need to give your kitty a nutritional supplement. The bottom line is that the nutrition a kitten gets will lay the foundations for future health!

2) What to feed adult cats and how often

Giving your cat small portions regularly helps it to control body heat, protects its digestive systems and lessens the risk of it becoming overweight.

Standard foods and diet

Eating canned cat food every day is not recommended. Many cat owners feel that canned food once or twice a week is more than adequate.

Also keep in mind that some canned foods are better than others. It's important to read the label on the tin to ensure that the contents do not contain sugar or inferior meats. Specifically look for canned foods that list meat or chicken as the first or second ingredient. Your cat's food should be served at room temperature.

Just like people, cats like variety in their diet. If you decide to change your cat's diet you need to do so gradually. Keep an eye on your cat and if there is any evidence of gastric problems you need to reconsider the food your Snowshoe is being given.

Dry food is a healthy option for your cat. Not only does it provide nutrition it may also help to keep your cat's teeth clean and its gums healthy if you get a correctly formulated food. Investing in a food dispenser is a good idea as it means that your cat can snack even when you are not around, day or night.

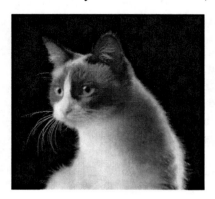

Just keep in mind that a cat that is eating more dry food will need to drink a lot of water. There must always be a good supply of fresh clean water available for you kitten or cat! Either there must be a bowl of water or you could invest in a more sophisticated option: a cat's drinking fountain.

Snowshoe cats love food and are keen to try anything. A word of warning, though: do not, I repeat not, give your cat human's food! This applies to scraps when you are cooking, treats from your plate during meals or leftovers. Firstly, your cat may be exposed to food stuffs that are toxic for him or her. Secondly, your cat will put on weight. Furthermore, you will end up with a cat that begs or even steals food.

Some Snowshoe owners believe very strongly in a diet that consists only of raw food and bones. Proponents of this diet state that their cats are healthier overall. Others think that any balanced, varied diet will be healthy. Yet other cat lovers believe that foods containing grains should be avoided. Again, when in doubt your best advisors will be the breeder your cat came from or your vet.

Preventative nutrition

Let's talk now about "preventative nutrition" which is the best kind of nutrition for your cat. If you think that your cat is "fine" and continue to give it foods that are not really recommended, there is a chance that it will at some stage develop serious health issues. For instance, cats that are constantly and exclusively given dry foods can suddenly develop the following conditions:

- Inflammatory Bowel Disease
- Asthma due to allergens
- Inflamed bladder
- Blocked urinary tract that, if severe, can led to rupture of the bladder and death
- Feline Diabetes
- Kidney stones.

These conditions can be prevented with a little attention to the food that your kitten and later your cat is given. As a pet owner, it is your responsibility to choose a diet that ensures longevity and long-term health benefits for your Snowshoe. In order to understand preventive nutrition, here are some things that you must learn about the nutritional requirements in cats.

Firstly, carbohydrates are very damaging to a cat's health. They cause diabetes, which is one of the most common diseases in domesticated cats these days. Cats are carnivores by design and nature, so feeding them on carbohydrates or plant-based proteins will upset their digestive system and potentially lead to more serious conditions or problems.

Secondly, the thirst drive is low in cats. It is therefore necessary for them to drink water along with their food. In the wild, the food that cats eat consists of almost 75% of water. Domestic cats will never make up for the lack of water by lapping from their water bowls. Water is extremely important to keep your cat healthy. If the cat's body does not receive the necessary amount of water there may be harmful repercussions such as urinary tract obstructions and / or infections. These problems are not common in cats that normally consume canned foods or other forms of wet food.

In addition, there are no benefits to the dental health of your cat from standard dry foods. There are some foods that have been specially developed by a manufacturer for cat's and their dental needs. These special – and sometimes expensive – foods are available from a vet.

However, there are some experts who claim that these foods that supposedly promote dental health don't actually work either because, although several dry food companies may claim this, there is no clear scientific basis to prove that this is true for cats. If you are unsure, approach a cat association or a third party whose only concern is cat's welfare.

In short, preventive nutrition is the only way to ensure that your Snowshoe has long lasting benefits from the food that it consumes. Of course, not all pet owners understand the principle that preventive nutrition is based upon. With reference to the understanding that you have acquired from the points mentioned above, here are the five principles of preventive nutrition that you can follow to ensure optimized and holistic nutrition for your cat:

- ✓ There must always be fresh water available
- ✓ Your cat needs to snack a great deal so food must always be available
- ✓ Provide a mixture of dry and wet or canned food
- ✓ Avoid foods that contain grains and carbohydrates
- ✓ Provide a balanced diet that is not too high in proteins or fats
- ✓ Ensure your cat is getting the vitamins and minerals it needs.

Food formulated by experts

Creating the right food for cats is not easy. There is a certain amount of expertise that is very important to ensure that all the key ingredients and nutrients are present in the formulae. There are specialized pet nutritionists who work to provide your cat with an optimized formula to ensure the correct nutrition. These foods are tested and tried for their effects before they are released for pet owners to use for their cats. There are several feeding trials that are conducted to understand how effective the formula is in enhancing the health of your cat.

According to association officials in America, feeding trials are the most important tools to understand the quality of a pet food. Those that have undergone feeding trials are given to the pets under recommended guidelines, which must be strictly followed to make sure that the cats get the right nutrition from them.

The quality controls involved in the development and testing of these foods begins with the concern with safety. There are several manufacturers that produce these foods in their own facilities and they are, generally, thought to be more trustworthy for a few reasons.

Firstly, the quality control is better as the source of the ingredients and all the associated processes are monitored effectively. All the foods that are manufactured on site are held until they meet all the safety guidelines recommended for the product. As a result, issues like Salmonella contamination are effectively prevented.

In addition, when you purchase a certain cat food, check if the food has been 'manufactured by' or just has been 'distributed by' the brand that you are choosing. If the brand that you are purchasing is made and distributed by the same company, it is easier to register complaints with respect to the quality of the food provided. You can report all the concerns that you have on the quality of the food to the manufacturer directly.

There are several brands and types of cat foods available and they are formulated for cats of various activity levels, ages and breeds. Some also help to prevent certain problems such as hairball formation.

There are several "life stage foods" that have been formulated because the nutritional requirements vary from kittens to adult and senior cats. However, there is another variety called the "ALL life stage" food that is available in some countries. This is definitely not widely recommended as it may lead to malnutrition or even excessive nutrition which could lead to several serious health issues in your cat.

If you find it hard to make a decision with regards to the right food choice for your feline friend, ask for help or advice from your vet or pet store salesperson. He or she should be able to help based on the breed and age of your cat.

3) What not to feed your Snowshoe cat

Usually cat owners think that their pets instinctively know what is best for them. Cats are can be picky eaters but there is little evidence that suggests that a cat knows what is right for it and what is wrong. Perhaps in the wild cats follow their instincts and get the right nutrition. However, with domesticated cats the varieties of foods that are available will make them interested in all the wrong sorts of things.

There are a number of food stuffs that should not be given to your Snowshoe or any cat for that matter:

- Onions, chives and garlic: at best your kitty's digestive system will be unhappy. At worst, eating onion regularly or a large amount can lead to anaemia.
- Milk and other dairy products: despite the clichés such as, "You look like the cat that ate the cream" and images of cats lapping milk, most cats are lactose intolerant.

- Caffeine: this can be fatal for cats. There is caffeine in tea, cocoa, carbonated drinks, many energy drinks and some cough and cold remedies. It is not only found in coffee.
- Chocolate: it contains theobromine which is highly toxic for cats and can lead to death. The darker the chocolate the more poisonous it is for cats.
- Liver: kittens especially shouldn't be fed liver as it is high in vitamin A. Too much of the vitamin can lead to severe bone problems and malformations.
- Raisins and grapes: for reasons that are still unclear, these can lead to kidney failure.
- Sweets/candy, diet foods and drinks, baked goods and some toothpaste: some of these contain the sugar substitute Xylitol which can cause liver failure in cats.
- Raw eggs: avidin, the protein in the egg white, inhibits the absorption of biotin, a vitamin necessary for skin health.
- Alcohol (yes, some – who don't deserve a pet – think it's funny to get a pet drunk): it has the same effect on a cat's brain and liver as it does on ours. The difference is that 3 teaspoons of whiskey will kill a 5lb or 2.3kg cat.
- Yeast dough: uncooked dough is never recommended for a cat. If your cat eats dough there is a chance that it will actually begin to rise inside the cat's stomach. During this expansion, the dough may stretch the stomach and abdomen causing pain or internal injury. In addition, the cat may suffer alcohol poisoning as the yeast ferments.
- Dog food: A bite once in a while will not harm your cat too much. However, the formula used in dog food is obviously for dogs and therefore definitely not suitable for cats. Cat food is packed with the proteins and vitamins necessary to fulfil a cat's nutritional requirements. On the other hand, dog foods may contain plant proteins that are not suitable for cats. If your Snowshoe regularly consumes dog food, it might become malnourished.

Often being cautious isn't enough and your cat might make its way into your kitchen or pantry and have a generous helping of restricted foods. There is no need to be unduly alarmed. Find out what it is that your cat has eaten and, in most cases, your vet will be able to provide an antidote to take care of the situation for you.

The golden rule is to stick to food and treats formulated for cats. No matter how much you think of your Snowshoe as a person, he or she is a cat. And be careful about what you leave within easy reach of your cat.

4) Treats

Treats are both a way of saying you love your cat and of rewarding good or desirable behaviour. While a game with you or a cuddle from you is probably what your Snowshoe likes the most, treats can be useful.

Using treats as part of an exercise routine can work, especially if you live in a smaller home or your cat is purely an indoor cat. You could hide a couple of dry treats around the house each day and your cat will get some exercise dashing about finding them. It is a good idea to start this routine when your Snowshoe is still young.

If you are unsure what treats are healthy for your cat, purchase them directly from your vet or you could ask the staff there for recommendations or suggestions. An alternative is to make your own treats by cooking up a little meat or chicken and giving your cat a small piece at a time.

Treats also don't have to be in edible form. What about a fun toy or some catnip?

Chapter 8: Grooming your Snowshoe

The Snowshoe is a short haired cat with a single layer coat. In other words, there is no evidence of an undercoat. The fur usually feels smooth to the touch. The short hair and lack of undercoat makes it easy to groom these cats despite the fact that the coat does undergo seasonal changes. The fur becomes thicker as the cold weather approaches and then your cat will lose some fur as the warmer months return.

When your cat is beginning to lose its winter coat it can be a good idea to brush it to help to remove the dead hair. Your cat will then swallow less fur. Most Snowshoes will groom themselves unless they are not feeling well or are stressed.

1) Bathing your Snowshoe

Unless your cat has managed to get itself particularly dirty somehow you will probably not find it necessary to bath your cat because he or she will keep itself well groomed and clean. Usually only cats that are ill, very old or stressed do not groom themselves.

However, if you decide to bath your Snowshoe I suggest that you get a number of things before you fetch your kitten or cat. You need to run warm or body temperature, *not* hot, water into the bathtub, basin, sink or container. The water should be body temperature or your cat may develop dandruff. As the water runs, add a small amount of shampoo to the water. Also, put a clean towel close by. Truly adoring cat owners will warm the towel slightly! Putting your cat into a bath or shower with you is not recommended.

Place your Snowshoe gently into the water and wet him or her using a cup, small jug or some other suitable receptacle. Once your cat is wet it is time for the shampoo. As with any animal, try not to get shampoo in your cat's eyes. Do not forget to wash the cat's bottom, feet and toes too.

Once you have rinsed off all the shampoo with clean water lift him or her out and wrap your cat in a towel. Talk soothingly to your cat throughout the bath if necessary. This is mandatory with most breeds but given Snowshoes quite like water you will probably be dealing with a relaxed cat anyway. Ending the bath and drying session with a treat of some kind in addition to praise and affection is a good idea!

2) *Nail care and clipping*

The warm water and shampoo will help to soften your cat's nails so do this part of grooming soon after bath time if you choose to bath your cat. If the nails need to be trimmed, use a small pair of fingernail clippers. Cut with care so as not to nick the skin or flesh around the nails. If your Snowshoe is a wriggler you must enlist help so that injuries are avoided.

3) *Ear care*

Use a cat-safe, gentle cleaning solution and good quality ear buds or Q-tips so that you don't deposit fibres and threads as you remove dirt. Warning: don't put the Q-tip or ear bud too deep into the ear as you will damage it and cause a great deal of pain.

4) *Tooth care*

Tooth or dental care is discussed fully in chapter 9 as it is a very important aspect of grooming and protecting the overall health and well-being of your cat.

5) *Products to use*

As with cat litter and food, there is a wide choice when it comes to cat-specific bath, cleaning or hygiene products. If you are unsure about what would be best, be guided by a breeder or by your vet when it comes to the best shampoo and so on.

The other items you will use are ones that people use too: ear buds or Q-tips, cotton wipes or swabs, mild baby wipes and fingernail clippers. Just be sure to buy good quality and hypoallergenic items.

Chapter 9: Your Snowshoe's health

The Snowshoe is generally a robust and healthy breed, although some cats may have a kinked tail or crossed eyes. These are both remnants of the Siamese heritage.

1) Finding a good vet

It is necessary for you to have a reliable vet who you can trust with your pet. It is never a good idea to constantly change the vet who treats your Snowshoe. Cats, as you know, do not appreciate change and most animals are reluctant to co-operate with vets. So, you must give your cat time to get accustomed to the scent, touch and voice of one vet.

Once your cat is comfortable with him or her, it will be more relaxed during visits to the vet. A vet is an important part of your cat's life and you must make sure you look for the perfect one to take care of your pet.

There will in all probability be several large and small veterinary clinics around your town or city area. As a result, there can be a huge choice, which can be confusing rather than helpful when you set out to choose one for your Snowshoe. The best way to look for a vet is to ask for recommendations from the breeder and your cat-owning friends and neighbours.

You must make an effort to look for someone who specializes in cat care. Alternatively, you can go to a vet practice that does at least have one or two vets who work mainly with cats. There are a few aspects that you might want to consider before you decide on a vet:

o   How far is the vet from your home?
o   Is the commuting time too long in event of an emergency?

- o Do you like the staff and find them confident and inspiring?

It is always better to find someone close to your house. It should preferably not take more than 15 minutes to drive down to your vet. Even if it is not an emergency, remember that your cat is not particularly fond of long drives. Once you have found someone who seems to fit into all the requirements, you can make a trial visit. The chemistry between your cat and the vet is extremely important if you want to make it a long-lasting relationship.

There are some signs that will indicate how comfortable you and your pet will be in a particular clinic. Make the following observations when you are visiting the vet for the first time.

- The waiting room must be clean and well maintained
- The ambience must be comforting for the cat so that it feels secure when it is being examined
- If it is a common clinic for dogs and cats, how are they housed when they are admitted for hospital care?
- The people at the reception must be friendly and helpful. They are going to be your point of contact in the coming sessions and you must be comfortable with them.

Once you are in the examination room, check how the vet interacts with both the animals and their owners. His or her tone must be soothing. The vet should be able to provide undivided attention to the animal being examined. He or she must also value your opinions about your cat's health, be willing to answer your questions and explain the situation with your cat, and must be respectful towards you and your feelings.

The personality of your vet plays an important part in the way he or she interacts with the animals being examined and treated. A vet must be genuinely passionate about his or her job. Without passion, you cannot be assured that a vet will go to all lengths to ensure the best for your Snowshoe.

The vet you select must be good with cats and have a complete and up to date knowledge of the different practices and techniques that have been developed in veterinary practice. He or she must also make a conscious effort to upgrade his or her skills and knowledge.

Once you are reassured about the behaviour of the vet towards you and your cat, you need to get down to the technical and legal aspects of choosing a vet.

- ✓ Is the facility equipped to handle emergencies?
- ✓ How many cages or rooms do they have for the pets that have been admitted?
- ✓ Are dogs and cats housed together?
- ✓ Is every staff member appropriately educated or trained?
- ✓ Is the facility licensed?
- ✓ What are the costs for tests and surgeries?
- ✓ Is the pricing competitive enough?
- ✓ What insurance policies do they accept?
- ✓ Are emergencies handled after regular working hours?
- ✓ Who takes care of the pets when they are hospitalized?
- ✓ Are they open to alternative medicines and treatments?
- ✓ Are the billing and administration systems reliable and accurate?

Once you've received satisfactory answers to all these questions, you can be assured that this facility is best suited for your cat. Remember, the person you choose as your vet is going to be your partner in the wellbeing of your Snowshoe for many years to come.

2) Preparing your cat for a vet visit

Taking a cat to the vet is not easy... for either of you! Cats experience a lot of stress when they are travelling. As a result, it is best that you prepare your cat well for a visit to the vet. Here are five tips that will make the visit less stressful for your cat:

The pre vet visit routine

Cats require a good amount of mental preparation before they are taken to the vet.

Start by giving your Snowshoe a thorough check up from head to toe. This is a more relaxed imitation of the examination that will take place in the vet's clinic. The idea is to get the cat used to being handled by the vet. Obviously in the event of an emergency this kind of preparation can't happen as there is no time.

Getting your cat used to the carrier is another way to making the visit less stressful. If your cat learns to associate the carrier with vet visits only, it might start to resist and fight being put into the carrier. On the other hand, if you create associations like play time or even outdoor visits with the carrier, your Snowshoe might look forward to the positive activities and be less stressed. You can also designate the carrier as a nap place. Throw in your cat's favourite toys and treats inside the carrier to attract it towards it.

Of course, the actual travel to the vet is going to create a great deal of stress in your cat. You can reduce this by being affectionate to him or her during the drive. Talk soothingly to him or her and, if possible, place the carrier in such a way that your Snowshoe can see you. This should reduce his or her anxiety levels.

Make your car cat friendly

Most cats dislike cars and some are very frightened by the noise and the smell. Much of the resistance to the visit to the vet is not the clinic itself but is more connected to the journey to the vet. Usually, cats are taken out in the car only during their visit to the vet. As a result, they automatically associate cars with the negative experiences that they have had at the vet including injections, pain, illness and bad tasting medicines. It's therefore hardly surprising that few cats stay calm and relaxed inside a car.

However, you can help your cat make positive associations by including drives in the car in your daily or at least weekly routine. You can take the car for short distances too. Take the car to the park, for instance. Then your Snowshoe will stop making negative associations. You can even stop by at the vet's clinic for 5 minutes to get your cat used to the staff there.

The basic idea is to get your cat used to the car. He or she must learn to be calm and relaxed during these visits. Keeping some toys in car and allowing your Snowshoe to play during these drives will also help a great deal.

Dealing with the waiting room

One place dreaded by all animals is the waiting room at the clinic. There are several unpleasant sounds like the barking of dogs, cats wailing and even chatter of humans that increase the levels of anxiety in a cat. There are also a lot of scary and unpleasant scents: dogs, other cats, unknown people, antiseptic, disinfectant and so on.

Cats are, by nature, solitary animals when they are not feeling well. Cats, regardless of whether they are well, sick, relaxed or stressed don't like being introduced to so many strange sights and sounds in one go. In addition, your Snowshoe is a sensitive, intuitive animal that will pick up fear in the other animals there. Animals can also discern ill health and pain in each other. The best thing to do would be to leave your cat in the carrier till he is called in for examination. This gives him a secure hide-out and he or she will be less anxious or frightened.

Make sure that the carrier that you are using is large enough. Place a nice cat bed or a cushion inside for him to rest. You can also leave toys and goodies inside the carrier. A top loading carrier is a must as it will become difficult or even impossible for you to get your frightened kitty out of a front loading one.

Special pheromone sprays are available to reduce anxiety and stress in cats during their visit to the vet. These sprays imitate the scent that cats leave when they rub themselves against the legs of their loved ones.

You can also schedule your more routine appointments to the less busy parts of the day. That way, the chaos in the waiting room will be reduced, making your cat feel more relaxed.

Get friendly with your vet

It is good to allow your vet to spend some time with your cat and break the ice. A good vet will take a few minutes to soothe a cat patient, and will give your Snowshoe a chance to sniff his or her coat and hands, for example.

Of course, the vet is going to have to poke and prod the cat during the examination. However, this becomes less stressful if the cat can look at the vet as a friend rather a stranger. Make sure you clear up all queries related to your cat's wellbeing when you visit your vet.

Send items from home

If your cat is scheduled for overnight hospital care or going to be admitted as a result of illness or injury, it can help if you send its favourite items from home, for example a blanket and a toy. The idea is to keep him or her around familiar scents, as this should reduce anxiety levels. There will, however, be times the vet won't allow this, as items from home will not be sterile.

Visits from you if your cat will be at the vet for an extended period may or may not reduce your cat's stress and anxiety levels. Your cat may just become distressed when you leave without him or her and confused about what is happening. Your vet will advise you about this.

You must always work with you vet to ensure the complete well-being of your cat. You must be able to trust the knowledge and expertise of your vet if you want him or her to be the best caregiver for your cat. Usually vets will be more than willing to lend support in the form of information or study material to help you understand how you can best take care of your cat at home.

3) Vaccinations

There is a range of vaccines for cats. They are placed into two groups: core and noncore.

The core vaccines protect against rabies, distemper, feline viral rhinotracheitis and feline calicivirus. These vaccines are given approximately every 3 years but more often in high risk areas. As with so much else, your vet will be your best guide.

Noncore vaccines are used based on a variety of factors such as breed, age, health status, the risk of exposure to certain diseases and how common a disease is in that area. In many instances cat associations recommend against these vaccines, such as FeLV for feline leukaemia. This is especially true for indoor cats.

The core vaccination timetable is:

> ➢ 6 – 7 weeks: Combination vaccine
> ➢ 10 weeks: Combination vaccine (distemper, rhinotracheitis and calicivirus) and Chlamydophila if necessary
> ➢ 12 weeks and older (governed by local laws): Rabies
> ➢ 13 weeks: Combination vaccine (distemper, rhinotracheitis and calicivirus) and Chlamydophila and Feline Leukaemia if the kitten is at risk of exposure.
> ➢ 16 and 19 weeks: Combination vaccine (distemper, rhinotracheitis, and calicivirus) and Feline Leukaemia if the kitten is at risk of exposure

> ➢ Adult cats: Combination vaccine (distemper, rhinotracheitis and calicivirus) and Chlamydophila and Feline Leukaemia if the cat is at risk of exposure.

If you acquired your kitten from a breeder the initial vaccinations will already have been done. It is vital that you keep up with them, particularly if your cat will be exposed to other cats or you live in a high risk area.

4) Neutering and spaying

As far as many are concerned, unless you are planning to breed with your Snowshoe you should have your cat spayed or neutered as soon as it is old enough.

Spaying is the surgical removal of the ovaries and uterus of a female cat. Neutering or castration is the surgical removal of the testicles from male cats. The hospitalization is brief, recovery is quick and the health and behavioural benefits last a lifetime!

The advantages for female cats are that they are far less likely to get breast cancer and will of course not contract uterine infections. In addition, they will no longer go into heat and indulge in activities like urinating and yowling to attract mates. This will help your pocket and your home.

With male cats, neutering prevents testicular cancer and means that your cat is far less likely to roam and therefore less likely to get into fights with other cats, be attacked by dogs or hit by a car.

In addition, the world has enough unwanted and homeless kittens. You don't want to have to home kittens that your Snowshoe produced after a minute or two of fun with the scruffy cat next door! As a pet owner one must take responsibility for the reproductive behaviour of one's pet.

To bust other myths, spaying and neutering will not make your cat fat, frustrated, crazed or depressed. Having this done is good for the cat, for you and for the community.

Best time for spaying

Snowshoe cats should ideally be spayed when they are 6-9 months old. In most shelters, this is the age when the Snowshoe is neutered or spayed before they are sent out for adoption. To reduce the chances of aggression and also pregnancies, make sure you schedule to have your Snowshoe spayed or neutered before it begins to mark its territory. This is when you know that your cat is physically ready to find a mate. It you have a female cat at home you must have her spayed to avoid any chance of her becoming pregnant.

In case you have neglected spaying or neutering, you can even take your cat to the vet when she is in heat. However, this can lead to excessive blood loss, which is certainly not desirable. If you think that you want your adult cat to be neutered or spayed, you can consult your vet about the safety of the procedure.

Behaviour changes after neutering or spaying

There is no apparent permanent change in a cat's personality after neutering or spaying. It is true that the cat might be quiet and subdued and not too playful for a while but he or she will get back to their usual self as soon as he or she recovers from the procedure.

You may have to provide your cat with a certain diet after neutering or spaying. This is to ensure that the cat gets all the nutrients and calories required during the recovery process. If you have any concerns about the process of neutering or spaying, your vet will be able to provide you with all the necessary details.

5) General early signs of illness

Naturally, the sooner you realise that your Snowshoe is not well the better as your cat will suffer less and treatment is more likely to be effective.

As you get to know your Snowshoe it will become increasingly easy for you to see when he or she is not well. Don't be concerned if your cat seems little off-colour for a day because that's fairly normal, but if the symptoms persist for two more days then you need to take action. Obviously if the symptoms are dramatic or severe or your cat has suffered an injury you need to take it to the vet immediately!

Behavioural changes to watch out for because they can be very good indicators of poor health include:

> Marked and sometimes sudden increase or decrease in appetite
> Extreme tiredness or lethargy
> Difficulty in standing or moving around
> Drinking far more water than usual
> Swelling of any part of the body or bloating of the abdomen
> Atypical behaviour such as aggression
> Difficulty with defecation or urination or the opposite (incontinence)
> Discharge from the nose, ears, eyes or any other body opening
> Excessive licking, scratching or biting at a part of the body.

Signs that your Snowshoe is in pain include crying, tilting or shaking their head in the event of ear pain, constant licking, limping dragging a limb, hissing if the painful area is touched, rubbing or pawing at an eye, and mouth pain that may cause increased salivation.

6) Common cat illnesses and health problems

Vomiting

Vomiting is a very common feline disorder. Usually cats vomit when they consume something that disagrees with them, is poisonous to some degree or an object that is not digestible. In addition to these situations, it can also be a symptom of some form of infection, diabetes or even a urinary tract disease.

Feline lower urinary tract infection

Almost 10% of cats get affected at the same stage in their lives by feline lower urinary tract infections. There are multiple causes for this group of disorders that affects both male and female cats. Most often it is stress related. In other cases, cats that eat fried foods might suffer from this condition. Feline lower urinary tract disorders are especially common in cats that are generally unhealthy, overweight or getting elderly.

The symptoms for feline lower urinary tract disorder include:

- The cat strains when urinating
- There are traces of blood in the urine
- The cat urinates in unusual places
- Loud purrs or cries while urinating
- Constant licking in the urinary area to reduce the pain
- Depression
- Sudden Dehydration
- Loss of appetite
- Constant vomiting.

The treatment for feline lower urinary tract infection depends on the cause and the type and degree of infection. The inability to urinate is a matter of great concern in pets. You must call your vet immediately if you observe one or more of the above symptoms.

Tapeworms

An internal infestation by tapeworms can be hazardous to your cat's health. These parasites usually invade the intestines of cats and can grow up to 2 feet in length if left untreated. Tapeworm infections have very subtle symptoms. This is why you must always keep a close watch on your cat to ensure that the problem of tapeworms does not go undetected. The symptoms include sudden weight loss even though the cat is eating, chronic vomiting and the presence of small white worms in the faeces and in the anal region.

The last symptom is an almost certain indication that a cat really is infected by tapeworms. This problem is usually linked with the presence of fleas on a cat because ingesting a flea can result in an infection by tapeworms. It is important to handle fleas as well when you are tackling the issue of tapeworms. The most common modes of treatment include tropical medication, oral medicines and injections.

Remember, too, that people can pick up tapeworms that can lead to infestations and even severe complications. Use a scoop or gloves when cleaning a cat box and wash your hands thoroughly.

Diarrhoea

Just as with other gastric upsets, there are several possible reasons for cats to develop diarrhoea. They range from those that are not a cause for real concern to serious conditions. The most common causes include a diet that is too rich, eating spoiled food, liver disease, allergies or food sensitivity such as lactose intolerance or cancer.

The biggest problem with diarrhoea is the danger of dehydration. It is therefore essential to give your cat plenty of fresh, clean water to drink to prevent this. Dehydration can lead to kidney and other complications that can be fatal if left untreated for too long.

You must also reduce the quantity of food you give to your Snowshoe for about 24 hours.

If the diarrhoea continues and is accompanied by a loss of appetite, lethargy, bloody stools and a fever you must take your cat to the vet as a matter of urgency for examination, diagnosis and suitable treatment.

Constipation

This is the most common digestive problem in domestic cats. A healthy cat will have a single, normal bowel movement a day. If your cat is constipated there is either a problem with its diet or there could be a more serious underlying health problem. Snowshoe cats that are more prone to constipation include overweight cats, elderly cats and those that have a low fibre diet and insufficient exercise.

Signs to watch out for include straining and crying when eliminating or trying to do so; small, dry and hard stools; stools that are covered in mucous or blood; frequent and unproductive trips to the litter box; loss of appetite; vomiting; weight loss; lethargy; signs of abdominal discomfort such as constant licking of their tummy; and a lack of general grooming. These are all indicators of a serious case of constipation and you need to consult a vet.

The causes of constipation include factors such as dehydration or insufficient fibre in the diet, an enlarged prostate gland in male cats, a blockage or abscess in the anal sacs, a side effect of a medication, a tumour or other obstruction in the intestine, an abnormality in the colon itself, diabetes, a hernia, obesity or a foreign object the cat swallowed that is causing a blockage.

Treatment will of course be determined by the cause of the cat's constipation. However, there are a number of stool softening and laxative products available for cats that are usually effective and easy to administer. Your vet may recommend a high-fibre diet for your Snowshoe and / or an increase in water consumption and in exercise. Avoid using liquid or medicinal paraffin.

In very severe cases a vet may have to perform an enema to flush out the colon or even perform a manual evacuation of the bowels. In the event of a tumour, hernia, obstruction or malformation surgery will be required.

Eye Problems

All cats have the potential to suffer from eye problems. The most common include conjunctivitis, retinal infections, bacterial and viral infections. Glaucoma and cataracts are age related eye problems that need to be taken care of as early as possible to preserve your cat's eye sight for as long as possible. Common symptoms of an eye problem are:

-   Cloudiness in the eye or eyes
-   Redness of the eyelid linings
-   Deposits in the corners of the eye
-   Eyes that are watery
-   Pawing at or rubbing the eye indicating pain or itching
-   Squinting
-   Keeping the eye closed or the inability to open it.

Standard preliminary treatment includes flushing the eye with water or a very mild saline solution and wiping away any deposits in the corner of the eye. If the problem continues, it is time to consult your vet.

Cats might also suffer injuries such as scratches to the eye if they are outdoors or have been in a fight. While very small scratches will heal on their own, marked or more serious eye injuries must be treated immediately!

Skin Problems

It's not always easy to spot a skin problem on a Snowshoe because of the dense coat. However, signs to watch for are excessive scratching, flakes of dry skin in the fur, marked hair loss or even bald patches.

If your kitten or cat develops a rash of small red dots or lumps on the skin it might be that he or she has had an allergic reaction to something. Your Snowshoe could be having a reaction to a wide range of things but the usual culprits are:

o Bacteria: your vet can identify the type involved and treat the infection easily
o Flea bites: there are various products available to deal with fleas
o Ear mites: these can be found on the body too, especially in kittens. A definitive diagnosis should be done by a vet
o Food or diet: like people, some cats are allergic to certain foods or ingredients
o Shampoo: you could try hypoallergenic products designed for human babies
o New medication: if this is the case your vet may be able to use an alternative treatment
o Water or food bowls or dishes: some cats react badly to plastic. You could use stainless steel, glass or ceramic containers instead
o Household cleaning products: if a cat comes into contact with one of these it will irritate and inflame the skin. If the reaction is severe, take your cat to the vet. Alternatively wash the affected area gently and use a soothing lotion
o New or different cat litter: cats quite often react badly to litters that are either perfumed or contain a lot of dust that is stirred up when the cat digs in the litter
o Burns and heat rash: these can be caused by sources of heat, chemicals or overexposure to sun. If the burn is severe, take your cat to the vet immediately for pain relief and to prevent infection.

You can't protect your Snowshoe from all potential allergens. Also, you won't know what he or she is allergic to until they come into contact. All a loving cat owner can do is take precautions to prevent or at least limit exposure to possible allergens and then take the right steps if a cat does have a bad reaction to something.

7) More serious conditions

Feline Infectious Peritonitis (FIP)

FIP is caused by infection of a cat by the Feline Coronavirus virus, which is very common in cats. However, often the only symptom will be mild diarrhoea. In rare cases the virus mutates and causes Feline Infectious Peritonitis. 80% of cats who contract FIP are younger than 2 years old.

Once a cat is infected, the virus spreads throughout the body and causes a range of symptoms including peritonitis, which is an accumulation of fluid in the abdomen. In some cases the fluid gathers in the chest cavity not the abdomen. In other cats the brain, eyes, liver, kidneys or other organs become inflamed.

Ordinarily, this virus mainly infects the intestinal tract, where it thrives and then replicates or multiplies. The virus is shed in the faeces and may survive in the outside environment for several days or even a few weeks. However, it is destroyed by common disinfectants. Infection is caused when a cat ingests the virus when grooming. Some cats will always be infected but they become immune to the virus. Other cats will become infected, recover and then be re-infected. In the majority of cases there will be no symptoms other than mild diarrhoea.

FIP is a very serious complication of a Feline Coronavirus infection. In this situation the virus no longer stays in the digestive tract; it mutates and spreads throughout the body. What is difficult is that none of the symptoms a cat will exhibit are unique to FIP. Early signs, for example, include lack of appetite, lethargy and a fluctuating fever. It can take anywhere from a few days to several months before other symptoms appear.

There are two forms of FIP: 'wet' or 'effusive' disease and 'dry' or 'non-effusive' disease. Cats often have a mix of these two types. With 'wet' FIP fluid collects in the abdominal or chest cavity. This results in distension and breathing difficulty respectively. The liquid that collects is due to damaged and inflamed blood vessels that leak fluid. 'Dry' FIP usually causes chronic lesions around blood vessels in various parts of the body, which lead to a type of inflammation. This inflammation can affect the eyes; the brain; tissues in the liver, kidneys, lungs and skin and even neurological disease.

Because symptoms are not unique to the disease, diagnosis is done on the basis of these symptoms and a battery of blood tests that look at white blood cell counts, protein levels in the blood, signs of jaundice or liver problems and liver enzyme levels. Often some of the fluid collecting in the abdomen or chest is analysed too.

A vet may also take X-rays or an ultrasound to assess fluid collection. Only if a combination of all these symptoms and results are found can a diagnosis be made. Another diagnostic option is a biopsy of affected tissue to examine it for the Feline Coronavirus virus itself. However, a cat is usually too sick for a procedure as invasive as this.

The disease is rapid and progressive. There is no cure for FIP and not much that can be done to ease the cat's suffering other than the use of anti-inflammatory drugs. Usually euthanasia is the most humane course of action to avoid suffering.

There is a vaccine that is available in some countries to help protect against FIP that can be given to kittens over 16 weeks of age. This vaccination is especially important in breeding households or where there are large groups of cats.

Feline Leukaemia Virus (FeLV)

Amongst cats in general, Feline leukaemia virus is the second leading cause of death in cats with the lead cause being trauma. This virus commonly causes anaemia (low red blood cells) or lymphoma (a group of blood cell tumours). It also suppresses the immune system, which leaves cats open to a host of infections. The good news is that about 70% of cats who contract Feline leukaemia survive.

Transmission is through saliva, blood, urine and faeces to a lesser degree. It is therefore most often spread during grooming or if an infected cat gets into a fight. It is not transmitted to people or dogs. Kittens can contract the virus before birth from an infected mother or after birth from her milk. Older cats are less likely to be infected; for some reason resistance increases with age. Indoor cats are far less likely to contract the virus.

The symptoms of Feline leukaemia include appetite and weight loss, diarrhoea, pale gums or yellowish colour in the mouth and eyes, fever, breathing problems, swollen glands, infections (skin, bladder or upper respiratory tract) and unsprayed females can become sterile.

This disease is diagnosed through a blood test, called ELISA, which is done by a vet. The test looks for FeLV proteins in the blood and is able to pick infection up in the early stages. The IFA blood test is used to detect the illness if it is at the advanced stage. If the result of this test is positive for the virus the outlook or prognosis for the infected cat is not good.

Unfortunately, 85% of the cats that suffer from a persistent FeLV infection will not survive for longer than 3 years. But, regular vet visits, care and good nutrition provide them with a good quality of life and guard against any secondary infections. These cats, though, must be kept indoors and spayed or neutered if they have not already been sterilised.

As you will have gathered, there is no cure for FeLV. Treatment is supportive and used to improve quality of life and fight secondary infections.

Feline Immunodeficiency Virus (FIV)

This virus is a complex retrovirus that leads to immunodeficiency disease in cats. In other words, cats infected with this virus can develop or maintain a normal immune response to protect themselves from infections.

This virus, which belongs to the same class as HIV that affects people, is a slow moving virus. It can also lie dormant in the cat's body for some time before there are any symptoms. Diagnosis is usually made when a cat is about 5 years old. The likelihood of infection increases with age. Males that roam are also more likely to be infected than males that don't and females. A cat can become infected through bites and scratches from an infected cat, in utero or when suckling from an infected mother, and – far less commonly – during sexual contact as the virus has been detected in semen.

The symptoms of FIV are diverse and can be confused with those for other illnesses. For instance, some of the infections these cats pick up are similar to those suffered by cats with Feline leukaemia virus. Recurring minor gastrointestinal and upper respiratory tract problems are common as are swollen or enlarged lymph nodes or glands. There can also be inflammation of the gums, especially the area of tissue around the teeth.

In more advanced cases there is upper respiratory tract disease and marked inflammation of various tissues including the eye, cornea, nose, glaucoma (increased pressure within the eyeball), persistent diarrhoea, chronic kidney problems and fungal infections affecting the cat's skin and / or ears. There is also usually fever and, as the disease progresses, marked weight loss. Certain types of cancers can develop, particularly in the lymphatic system, and changes to the nervous system can cause disrupted sleep and behaviour patterns, increased aggression in some, loss of hearing and disorders that affect the nerves in the cat's legs and feet.

Diagnosis of FIV is achieved by taking a detailed medical history, doing a thorough examination, blood tests including a blood profile and count and analysing the cat's urine. Before a final diagnosis is made, a vet must rule out parasites, tumours and infections caused by bacteria, fungi or other viruses.

Treatment of a cat with Feline immunodeficiency virus takes place on an outpatient basis unless the cat is dangerously dehydrated. The first job for the vet is to deal with secondary infections before they become serious or cause complications. If necessary, surgery is done to remove tumours and badly infected teeth. Cats living with this illness will also be placed on a specifically formulated diet.

As an owner of a cat with FIV one needs to watch one's cat for recurring or additional secondary infections or any other symptoms. A cat must also be kept on its special diet and seen regularly by a vet. If the diagnosis is made fairly early, cats with this illness can live long and relatively healthy lives.

The main focus of prevention is a vaccination. In addition to this, keeping your cat indoors and away from cats that are or may be infected is the second line of defence.

Hyperthyroidism

Hyperthyroidism or an overactive thyroid gland is a common disorder, particularly in cats over the age of seven, and affects both males and females. The thyroid glands in the neck increase their production of the hormones that regulate many of the body's processes. When there is too much of the hormone the effects and symptoms can be severe. Some cats become seriously ill, but fortunately most cats that develop this condition can be treated and recover fully.

The cause of the condition in over 70% of cats is a benign or non-cancerous change in the thyroid glands. At this stage it is not clear what brings this change about. Unlike humans who only have one thyroid gland, cats have two of these glands. With this change in the older cat's body the glands become enlarged in addition to producing too much hormone. In a very small number of cats (1 to 2%) the disease is caused by a cancerous tumour in one or both of the glands.

Symptoms appear gradually and, if the condition is not treated, worsen over time. One of the body systems or processes the thyroid controls is metabolic rate. Cats suffering from this problem burn energy too fast and therefore get very thin despite being hungry and eating a lot. In addition to constant hunger and weight loss, other symptoms are a marked increase in thirst levels, greater activity that can appear more like restlessness, irritability, increased heart rate and the coat looks uncared for and there may be hair loss. In more severe cases cats become very heat sensitive or intolerant, will develop diarrhoea and vomiting and may even pant. There can also be weakness and lethargy.

If hyperthyroidism is left untreated it is potentially lethal for a cat, as there can be complications. Cats can develop hypertension or high blood pressure. Untreated raised blood pressure can damage the kidneys, eyes, brain and the heart itself. The increased heart rate causes changes in the muscles of the heart wall. Eventually this can lead to heart failure. Medication is needed to control the blood pressure.

Although this condition usually results in enlarged glands they are rarely visible. A vet will be able to detect it when he or she does a careful examination. However, a check up is not always enough so blood tests are also used. The primary test measures the level of thyroid hormones (thyroxin or T4) in the blood. A further blood test that is sometimes required examines liver enzymes and liver health. A vet will also often perform a urine test to check kidney function, measure blood pressure and – in severe cases – a chest x-ray or an ultrasound.

The good news is that with treatment all the signs and symptoms disappear. Periodic blood tests are performed, though, as the condition does not go away. The vet will monitor thyroxin levels and kidney function on an ongoing basis. There are currently four main treatment options:

➢ *Medication*: The most commonly used and effective anti-thyroid drugs are in the group called thioamides, which includes both methimazole and carbimazole. Both are widely used in the management of feline hyperthyroidism. These drugs reduce the production and release of thyroid hormones and so control the illness. They are not a cure but they are effective and safe.

To control the disease the medication must be given daily and often twice daily. While side effects are uncommon they can include decreased appetite, lethargy and vomiting. The side effects stop after the first few weeks of treatment. More serious side effects are extremely rare.

➢ *Surgical thyroidectomy*: The surgical removal of the affected parts of the thyroid glands can result in a cure. As a result it is a common treatment for many hyperthyroid cats. However, occasionally signs of hyperthyroidism develop again at a later stage because thyroid tissue that was not diseased before is affected.

To reduce anaesthetic and surgical complications, cats are ideally stabilised with anti-thyroid drug therapy before surgery is carried out. If the cat is suffering from heart disease this must also be addressed before the procedure. The major risk associated with the surgery itself is accidentally damaging the parathyroid glands, which are small glands close to or even inside the thyroid glands. The parathyroid glands are essential to maintain stable blood calcium levels.

Because there is a small risk of temporary interference with calcium regulation postoperatively, cats usual remain hospitalised for a few days after surgery. The cat's overall health and recovery and monitored in addition to the blood calcium concentrations. Occasional blood tests are recommended by vets in order to ensure that normal thyroid hormone levels are being maintained.

➢ *Radioactive iodine therapy*: Radioactive iodine (I-131) sounds scary but it is a very safe and effective treatment for hyperthyroidism. The first benefit is that it is usually a once-off treatment and – in most cases – a permanent cure. In fact, a single injection cures in the region of 95% of all cats suffering from hyperthyroidism.

The radioactive iodine is administered as an injection that is given under the skin. The iodine is only absorbed by the abnormal thyroid tissue. The radiation then destroys the affected thyroid tissue but it does not damage any of the surrounding tissues or the parathyroid glands.

There are no significant side-effects with this treatment, but because the cat is temporarily radioactive it must, as a precaution, be kept at the clinic or vet for a short time after treatment. It is recommended that occasional blood tests are done after treatment to make sure normal thyroid hormone levels are being maintained.

➢ *Dietary treatment*: A new and more recent option for the management of hyperthyroid cats is to feed them on a special diet with strictly controlled levels of iodine. The logic behind this is that iodine is used by the thyroid gland to make thyroid hormones. If there is only enough iodine in the cat's diet to make normal levels of thyroxin the disease can be controlled.

This is a new and so far promising new treatment. It does mean that the owner must exclusively feed the cat a special therapeutic diet that is only available from a vet.

If a cat's hyperthyroidism is caused by a malignant, cancerous tumour (a thyroid adenocarcinoma) then treatment is far more difficult and success is less certain. Treatments involving very high doses of radioactive iodine have shown good results.

Feline diabetes mellitus

There are two types of diabetes mellitus in cats and they are not the same as the types of diabetes found in people.

The first is Type I or Insulin-dependent Diabetes Mellitus (IDDM). This is the form of diabetes that affects 50 to 75% of diabetic cats. The cause of IDDM is the loss of beta cells in the pancreas. These cells produce insulin and without them a cat must have insulin treatment or it will die. Cats with this type of diabetes are often very thin and they can develop serious conditions (ketoacidosis) because of the body's inability to use fat instead of glucose for energy.

Type II is Non-insulin-dependent Diabetes Mellitus (NIDDM). This affects the remaining 50 to 25% of cats with diabetes. Unlike with IDDM, these cats still have beta cells in the pancreas but the insulin response to a high blood sugar or glucose level is not normal. With this type there is a delay in insulin secretion when the blood glucose starts to increase, followed by excess insulin secretion. The cells of the body also do not react normally to insulin. Cats with NIDDM survive without additional insulin but therapy is often used to ease the symptoms and maintain weight control. Some cats with NIDDM can be successfully treated with diet changes. Cats with type II diabetes are usually overweight and rarely need insulin to survive. The danger with this type is that the beta cells may die and the cat could progress to IDDM.

Some cats develop Secondary Diabetes Mellitus. This happens when another illness results in the destruction of or damage to beta cells in the pancreas. Some of the illnesses that can cause secondary diabetes are hyperthyroidism, Cushing's disease, pancreatitis or acromegaly (a production of too much growth hormone). The cat may or may not need insulin treatment depending on how serious the damage to the pancreas is. In addition, secondary diabetes is reversible in some cases.

There are various signs and symptoms of diabetes mellitus in cats:

➤ *Increased thirst and urination*: glucose can't enter the cells so levels in the blood become far too high. The kidneys then filter out the glucose. Because the cat urinates more it needs to drink more.

➤ *Inappropriate elimination*: the fact that the cat is urinating more often means that there may be accidents in the house. Diabetic cats are also prone to urinary tract infections, which can also lead to urination outside a litter box.

➤ *Appetite changes*: some diabetic cats eat less because they don't feel well. Other cats suddenly eat far more than before.

➤ *Weight loss*: due to the illness the cat can't use the calories consumed for energy. Instead body fat is broken down and used as fuel for the body. As fat is used the cat becomes thinner.

➤ *Change in gait*: the disease can result in nervous system abnormalities, which makes the cat walk with their hocks almost touching the ground. Vets call the condition causing this strange almost crouching gait diabetic neuropathy.

➤ *Weakness, lethargy and depression*: the cat feels weak and without energy because he or she is unable to use the food it eats. Some diabetic cats also lose muscle and this contributes to weakness. If the cat is also depressed it may well stop grooming and no longer be interested in things around it.

➢ *Vomiting*: cats with severe diabetes that are breaking down the fat in their own bodies for energy have waste products – called ketones – that begin to accumulate as a result. Ketones in the blood cause nausea and vomiting. If the level of ketones in the blood gets very high and the pH drops, this increase in acidity leads to a life-threatening condition called ketoacidosis.

Common symptoms of ketoacidosis are loss of appetite, vomiting, diarrhoea, weakness, change in respiration, dehydration, and sometimes collapse. In severe cases, you will be able to smell acetone on the cat's breath. A cat suffering ketoacidosis is an emergency case and no time should be lost. These cats require around the clock care and monitoring. Treatment will involve insulin, intravenous fluids, medications that reduce potassium levels to normal and sometimes antibiotics are also needed because these cats are very prone to infections.

Diagnosis of feline diabetes mellitus is based on the presence of persistently high blood glucose levels (hyperglycaemia) even when the cat has not eaten recently, glucose in the urine (glycosuria) and common signs and symptoms. Symptoms alone are not enough because they are similar to those found with kidney failure and hyperthyroidism. Diagnosis consists of several aspects:

➢ A full medical history
➢ A thorough physical examination
➢ Blood and urine tests.

The blood and urine tests are usually done more than once, as the glucose levels need to be persistently high for a diagnosis to be made. The tests also look at liver enzymes, raised cholesterol, and whether the levels of sodium, potassium and phosphorous are lower than normal.

A classification of insulin-dependent, non-insulin dependent or secondary diabetes cannot be clearly made for some cats. This is because there is a spectrum of disease that ranges from severely insulin dependent, to requiring small doses of insulin, to requiring none. In addition, the insulin-dependence of a cat might change over the course of its life as it moves slowly from, for example, non-insulin-dependent diabetes to insulin-dependent diabetes. There are also some cases of transient diabetes where a cat needs insulin for a while and then, after a few months or even a year, they no longer need this treatment.

8) Obesity in Snowshoe cats

In case of medium sized cats like the Snowshoe, the effect of being overweight or obese on their health and general well-being is always negative. Besides the usual problems like sluggishness and lethargy, obesity in cats has several associated health disorders. Snowshoe cats are mainly indoor cats. This means that they need constant stimulation to keep themselves active. If your cat is unable to get the amount of exercise that he requires, be prepared to deal with 'weighty' cat issues.

Sometimes it becomes very difficult to determine if your cat is overweight. Obesity is harder to miss! Just because the cat's levels of activity and agility seem to be fine doesn't mean that it is not chubbier than it should be. There are reliable ways of telling if your cat is becoming obese. You can try three simple tests at home before you have an actual expert test your cat for obesity.

How to tell if your Snowshoe is overweight

Step number one is to feel the area around the rib cage of your cat. If you are still able to feel the rib cage through his or her fur, it means that he or she is not obese. However, if you have to press really hard to get to the rib cage, it means that your cat is heavier than the normal, acceptable weight.

Secondly, a cat's waistline should have a distinct shape: the body tapers from the belly towards the hind quarters. If a cat is too tubby and the body extends evenly from belly to the rear quarters and pelvis, it is a sign that your cat needs to lose weight.

A hanging pouch between the hind legs of a cat is a definite indication of the cat being overweight. If the pouch is more like a flap of skin rather than a fat-filled pouch it probably means that your older cat was too fat, lost the weight but the skin had stretched.

Like humans, cats that are overweight will experience several health issues. Therefore, you must take the necessary measures to slim your cat down and maintain a healthy weight.

Obesity related health problems

One of the most common complaints in veterinary clinics across the globe is health disorders related to obesity. The biggest threat to the wellbeing of cats is feline diabetes mellitus. The second most prevalent disorder in cats due to obesity is hyperthyroidism, which is due to excessive production of thyroid.

According to experts, the chances of an obese cat becoming diabetic are double in comparison to cats that have a normal weight. This risk becomes 8 times higher if the cat becomes severely obese. The association between obesity and diabetes is quite evident. When your cat becomes obese, there is a drastic increase in the amount of inflammatory markers and oxidative stress. This causes insulin resistance, which leads to obesity.

The resistance to insulin is one of the most common problems found in cats. It has also been observed that a change in diet is not as effective in increasing insulin sensitivity as the actual reduction in weight.

There are several other health conditions that can be found in cats due to feline obesity:

Osteoarthritis and lameness: This condition occurs because there is too much stress on the medium sized frame of your Snowshoe. You will be able to hear loud thuds when your cat jumps off a table or chair, which indicates a gradual loss of agility in the cat.

Liver and urinary system: Too much pressure on the liver also causes liver problems like feline lipidosis syndrome. Also, urinary tract disorders are common in cats that are obese.

The biggest issue with obesity is not the condition itself. The inability of many owners to recognize this condition and provide necessary treatment is the cause for the drastic increase in feline obesity in the last couple of years. There are many cases that have been reported where owners are just used to over-feeding their cat. They actually think that normal sized cats look malnourished and unhealthy.

As the owner, it is your responsibility to evaluate the condition of your cat's body on a regular basis. You can also get a body condition score to check for the amount of fat present in your cat's body. These scores show the difference in the calorie intake of your cat and the actual energy requirement. If your Snowshoe is being overfed, the score will go up to indicate an increase in fat deposits.

How to keep your Snowshoe at a healthy weight

It is actually not very difficult to maintain your cat's normal body weight. All you need to do is ensure that the width of the hips and shoulders are maintained without any visible bulge on the sides. You must also make sure that the belly of your cat does not hang too low.

Since the Snowshoe is a slender but muscular cat by nature, fat deposits do not always become clearly evident early on. Once you have spotted it there are fortunately a few things you can do to reduce obesity in your cat.

Firstly, you need to understand what the right amount of food for your cat is. The quantity of food that you give your cat should be just enough to keep it healthy. It is impossible to quantify the amount of food that one should give a Snowshoe as the cat's age, gender, state of health, activity levels etcetera all impact on this. However, you can measure the calorie intake in your cat if need be. Your vet or a local breeder or association can advise you as to how many kilocalories per kilo of body weight your cat should be getting.

Depending on your cat's health, you can determine how much food it requires. If there has been any recent surgical procedure or neutering / spaying, you must make sure you reduce the food intake accordingly.

Free choice feeding is a very common problem. Cat owners, out of love, provide their cat with a range of flavours and choices. This often leads to over eating. In addition, if you mix dry cat food with canned food there is a chance of overeating. Similarly, constant changes in the taste of foods will make your cat overeat because of the novelty. Like us, cats find it hard to resist a great tasting meal.

Using a measuring cup to judge portion size and so ensuring that your cat is neither over fed nor under fed can be very helpful. However, if you prefer free choice feeding, divide the food into two portions. Give your cat one helping in the morning and one in the evening. You must also be very careful that the feeding is age appropriate. Depending on whether you have a kitten or a senior cat in your household, the choice of diet will vary.

The importance of keeping your cat hydrated can't be stressed enough. You must make sure that there is plenty of fresh water available for your cat, especially if you are feeding it dry cat food, While most dry foods work very well for cats, lack of water might lead to issues like urinary tract disorders and also lowered kidney function.

Water is an essential nutrient for your Snowshoe. Irrespective of whether you are feeding it wet or dry food, you must give it enough water. The presence of adequate amounts of water in the body will help your cat process and absorb the food that it has eaten. Proper digestion and elimination, which is the key to good health in a cat, is regulated by the amount of water available.

If you have put your cat on a weight loss diet, you must give him adequate amounts of protein. It is true that the calorie intake must be restricted. However, you must always make sure that you do not reduce the amount of essential nutrients. When you increase the amount of proteins, weight loss is aided while keeping the lean body mass intact.

If you are concerned about the weight and health of your Snowshoe, make sure you reduce the amount of treats and titbits. This practice must be extended to at least a couple of weeks after the 'diet' period. You must make sure that everyone in your family is aware of this rule.

If you try and cheat out of affection, remember that you are harming your cat's health. It would help, instead, to cut your cat's meals down to smaller, more frequent meals. This will ensure that it does not experience hunger pangs while continuing to stay on a healthy diet.

Crash diets are as harmful for cats and they are for humans. You must never starve your cat. In fact, no matter what restrictions you make in its diet, it must be supervised by a dietician. If you don't carefully monitor the amount of minerals and vitamins your cat is getting it can lead to a fatal condition called hepatic lipidosis, which affects the liver.

Exercise is extremely important in cats. You cannot control the health and weight of your Snowshoe by only altering its diet. You must also ensure that it has an active lifestyle. This means that you will be both controlling the calories your cat takes in and making sure that he or she burns the calories through exercise and activity. One can do a number of things to encourage activity and to keep your cat's environment stimulating and engaging.

To begin with, set aside a dedicated time to play with your cat or cats. You can use simple toys like strings to help your Snowshoe play and get a good workout. (You will probably get one too)!

In addition, allow his or her natural instincts to take over; let your cat climb, jump, pounce, scratch and even chase around the house. These exercises are interesting and fun for your cat and will increase the process of weight loss.

It is suggested that cat owners get a feeding ball to give a cat one meal in the day. The advantage with the feeding ball is that your cat will have to put in some effort to roll the ball and get to the food inside.

Also, you could place your cat's food bowl at the top of a flight of stairs. This will encourage your Snowshoe to climb to get to the food.

Throughout the process of weight loss, you must be extremely patient. It will take several weeks and even months for your cat to lose weight. If you find it too hard to maintain the weight of your cat on your own, you can ask your vet for tips. You could even enrol your Snowshoe in a veterinary weight loss clinic for additional support and information.

9) How to give your Snowshoe medication

Giving medication to a cat can be a challenge. One needs to try and do so in a way that will not stress or hurt your cat… or you!

In order to give your Snowshoe a pill or tablet, hold your cat against your body and on a surface that is about waist height to you. Place the thumb and fingers of one hand on either side of your cat's mouth. If you press gently with your fingers and tilt the cat's head back, its mouth should open automatically. Using your other hand, gently pull the lower jaw down and place the pill or tablet as far back on the tongue as you can. Continue to hold the head back and keep your cat's mouth closed until you are sure that he or she has swallowed the medication. When you let go watch your cat for a minute or so in case he or she spits the pill out.

If you need to give a liquid medication, tip the cat's head back. Open his or her mouth as you would if you were going to be administering a pill or tablet. Then gently pull out a corner of the lower lip to form a pocket. Pour the liquid medicine into the pocket in the lip and then hold your cat's mouth closed until he or she has swallowed. Don't try to administer so much at once that most of the dose is spilled before it has a chance to go into the mouth.

If you need to restrain a cat, for whatever reason, wrap it in a soft blanket with only the part of the cat you need to deal with exposed. Make sure that it is tight enough to prevent the cat escaping easily but not so tight that it causes pain or discomfort.

10) How to clean your cat's teeth

Like any other cat, the Snowshoe is susceptible to problems with its teeth and gums. The most common of these is gingivitis or gum inflammation.

This condition is caused by the build up of plaque mixed with saliva and food particles on the teeth. If this substance hardens into tartar and builds up along the gum line the gums become inflamed and even infected. This can cause pain and bleeding and your cat may find eating painful. If periodontal disease goes unchecked your cat will eventually lose his or her teeth.

The vet can remove tartar by using a procedure known as descaling. However, if you practice good dental hygiene from the time your Snowshoe is a kitten you can avoid any serious oral or dental diseases.

It is very important that you begin to clean your Snowshoe's teeth when he or she is still a baby. This way, at least your cat will be used to it even though it will never enjoy it. It is best to clean a cat's teeth daily. The absolute minimum is twice a week.

The best way to handle the dental routine is to collect all the supplies you will need in advance before you tackle your cat. Some cat owners use sterile gauze strips to clean their cat's teeth. Others begin with gauze and move, as their cat becomes more tolerant, to a soft rubber toothbrush. You can buy toothbrushes and toothpaste from your vet. Please note that you should never under any circumstances use toothpaste that is designed for people as this could be very dangerous, even fatal, for your cat!

In order to get a kitten used to the sensation of having something in its mouth, you can begin by just using your little finger, which you have dipped into something the kitten will enjoy the taste of. For example, you could use the brine solution that tinned tuna comes in. Once your kitten has become used to this, begin to wrap gauze around your finger which also has been soaked in the solution the kitten will like. To begin with, only clean one or two teeth in a session and then gradually increase the number of teeth you work on.

In order to clean your kitten or cat's teeth, either wrap a strip of gauze around your index finger or use the toothbrush. Dip either the gauze or toothbrush into the feline toothpaste a saline solution. With the cat on your lap, gently open its jaw and rub your finger or the toothbrush on each tooth using a circular motion. You need to pay particular attention to the areas next to the gum where tartar builds up. You need to be thorough but gentle enough that you do not damage the gums.

As with all the hygiene and health care procedures you do with your cat you must remember to make comforting sounds and talk soothingly to him and her while you were working. Afterwards you need to praise him or her and make time for cuddles and even playing a game. Your cat should enjoy the rewards so much that he or she is willing to endure this hygiene routine in order to have the fun afterwards!

11) The self-medicating cat

We've all seen cats eating grass and many of us assume that it is something they do when their tummies aren't feeling quite right. All cats eat grass, but the experts are not entirely sure why.

Eating grass certainly seems to help cats that need to regurgitate hair they have swallowed. A considerable amount of grass consisting of whole blades does have an emetic effect. It is also possible that when they just nibble at the tips of grass cats are taking in the roughage that they feel they need in order to regulate their digestive systems. Another theory is that they get additional trace elements and vitamins from grass and they instinctively know when they need them.

Whatever the reason, it appears that cats need and want to eat grass on occasion. If you don't have a garden or your cat is purely an indoor cat you will need to plant a window box or a pot with suitable grass for your kitty to snack on.

12) De-clawing a cat

In a word: don't! The process of de-clawing a cat involves the surgical amputation of the first joint of every digit on the cat's front feet. In other words, it is a mutilation of the cat that causes considerable post-operative pain and possible phantom pain the rest of its life. If you train your cat properly and supply it with a scratching post there is absolutely no acceptable reason to have this procedure done.

This practice is followed in order to prevent the cat from damaging furniture and property. Other pet owners also justify declawing a cat as a method of protecting other people from being scratched or hurt by their cat. In some residential properties, people are not allowed to keep cats unless they are completely declawed.

It is quite certain that those who advocate declawing do not understand the seriousness of this procedure. It is not a way of keeping the nails trimmed or blunt. It is a medical surgery that has horrible repercussions for the cat. It is permanent and irreversible. There is also no guarantee that your Snowshoe will ever recover entirely from this traumatic experience. For this reason, several European countries have strong laws against declawing the cat.

If you have considered declawing or had it suggested to you, remember that the toes and claws are an important part of the anatomy of the cat which makes it more agile and graceful. The claws allow cats to get purchase on surfaces. Declawing also deprives a cat of its instinctive defence mechanism: the ability to climb a tree to escape danger at ground level and to also to use its claws to scratch an attacker and defend itself.

The recuperation period following de-clawing is very hard and painful. The short-, medium- and long-term impact on the cat is significant.

For up to three days after the surgery, the cat will suffer post procedure lameness and will drag itself around. A cat will not lose its instinctive behaviour even if it is in pain. It will therefore still need to walk, jump and scratch despite the pain. It will also have to use the litter box. This will impact on recovery time.

Almost 80% of cats that have undergone declawing have developed complications after surgery or even after discharge that were caused by the wrong sheering techniques being used or even the nature of the blade used for surgery. The most common conditions include abscesses, necrosis (death) of tissue, growth of deformed claws, motor paralysis, nerve damage, haemorrhage, stress induced bladder inflammation, infections, swelling and even reluctance to walk.

Furthermore, there have been reports that declawing can change the cat's personality including that of cats that were previously loving and gentle:

> The biting frequency and strength increases in most cats. The only possible explanation to this is that when a cat loses one form of defence, it activates another.
> House soiling is twice as common in declawed cats. Firstly, they become reluctant to walk and put pressure on their paws. In addition to that, severe cases like nerve dysfunction and even lameness leave the cat helpless.
> Aggression is very common in cats post declawing. The pain makes them more defensive against people. Also, the fact that you, their owner and the person who should take care of and protect them, inflicted that pain on him or her makes you less trustworthy in the eyes of your cat and the cat generally less trusting and far more anxious.

Almost 45% of cats in America that have been declawed are referred to vet teaching hospitals and cat schools to sort out behavioural issues. The change in behaviour is more drastic if the cat has undergone tendonectomy in the process of being declawed. The repercussions of these behaviour changes include relinquishing cats to shelters. For a cat like the Snowshoe, which gets particularly attached to people, this experience is extremely traumatic.

There are alternatives to declawing a cat.

✓ Trim your cat's nails with a nail clipper. This will reduce the damage caused by your cat's claws to a large extent.

✓ Another simple option is to provide your cat with a scratching post. You can attract your cat to the scratching post by using scent sprays that smell like catnip. A sisal scratch post is most recommended for cats as the roughness of the surface is just right for the cat to fulfil its urge to scratch something.

✓ One of the simplest and most effective solutions are nail caps made of vinyl that you can simply glue to the front claws of your cat. It is best recommended for those who have cats like the Snowshoe that spend a lot of their time indoors. You can even protect your children from the cat with the help of "Soft Claws" or a similar product available from a vet or good pet shop. Once these caps wear off, they can be simply replaced with a new set.

✓ Train your cat. That is the best way to protect your space and others from the claws of the cat. Teach your cat to only use the scratch post. You can also train it to be at its best behaviour when it is around strangers.

For a cat like the Snowshoe all of these alternatives work well. In case your cat is in the habit of venturing outside, you might want to avoid clipping the nails or even using nail caps so that your cat can be on guard.

13) A first aid kit for your cat

First aid items for your cat should be stored in a suitable container that is easily accessible, portable and clearly marked. It is also recommended that a feline first aid kit should include the following items although others can of course be added if you find them useful:

- o Antibiotic powder
- o Antiseptic wash
- o Cat laxative
- o Eye dropper
- o Gauze swabs
- o Hydrogen peroxide 3%
- o Mercurochrome
- o Roll of cotton wool or absorbent cotton
- o Roll of adhesive bandage (2.5 cm or 1" wide)
- o Roll of adhesive bandage (7.5 cm or 3" wide)
- o Roll of gauze bandage (2.5 cm or 1" wide)
- o Sharp, pointed scissors
- o Round tip scissors
- o 20 ml plastic syringe
- o Thermometer
- o Anti-bacterial and anti-fungal solution such as tincture of iodine
- o Torch or flashlight
- o Tweezers.

In order to maintain the kit, you will need to clean any instrument that you have used before putting it back in the kit. If any of the consumables are used, replace them the same day.

It is also advisable to check the kit contents every six months to ensure that everything is in order, nothing has expired and that the batteries in the torch or flashlight still work.

14) Preparing your cat for surgery

No matter what surgical procedure your cat is going to undergo, a good amount of preparation is mandatory. You can get all the necessary pre surgical advice from your vet. Make sure you adhere to all the guidelines.

The most common precaution to take is to ensure that your cat does not eat anything after midnight until the surgery. If you are taking a kitten for operation, on the other hand, the nutritional requirements are drastically different and you should ask your vet for guidance.

Following these measures will at worst reduce the chances of complications and, at best, ensure that there are no complications during the surgery, immediately following it and later on during the recuperation phase after your Snowshoe has left the animal hospital.

15) The recovery process

Your Snowshoe will experience discomfort to some or other degree after the procedure. If your cat is in pain, you must make sure you either leave it under specialized care or consult your vet regularly. There are a few precautions that you can take to ensure that the recovery process is comfortable and safe.

- Give your cat a safe, quiet place in the house to rest during the recovery process. This place should not be accessible by other pets or even children.
- Do not encourage jumping, running or playing during the recovery process. You can take your Snowshoe out on sedate, short walks but make sure that it doesn't get physically overexerted or too tired.
- The area that has been operated on should not be licked. So, getting your cat an Elizabethan collar is the best option although the vet will probably put one on anyway.

- During the recovery process, avoid using litter or sand / soil in the litter box and rather use shredded paper. The problem with sand or litter is that the dust generated when your cat digs in it can get into a wound and cause infections or irritation.
- The site of the incision must be cleaned regularly to avoid infections.
- Look out symptoms at the site of the incision:
  o Redness
  o Swelling in the site of the incision
  o Discharge from the area
- Reduced appetite
- Vomiting
- Lethargy

If you do notice one or more of these symptoms, you need to inform your vet immediately.

Chapter 10: Behavioural issues

Your cat's health must be your priority. You can ensure that your Snowshoe stays healthy by taking it for regular vet visits, providing it with nutritious food and also ensuring that it gets enough exercise. Most physical health issues can be treated quite easily. However, if you see sudden behaviour changes in your cat, it could be suffering from some psychological disorder.

1) Sleeping habits

One of the things cats do best is sleep. On average, a healthy adult cat spends 16 or even more out of every 24 hours asleep. In other words, they spend two thirds of their time sleeping. Scientists and researchers are not quite sure why cats sleep so much.

Cats will have shorter naps and long sleeps throughout the day. No two cats will have the same sleep routines any more than people do. Sleep patterns are also affected by the weather, the cat's age, how relaxed its feeling, its general state of health, whether it's hungry or not and what its human companion is doing.

There is a fair amount of anecdotal evidence that suggests that cats are more likely to sleep when their people are not there or unavailable. Domestic cats often seem to adjust their sleep patterns in accordance with the daily rhythms of its owner and the household it lives in.

All cats will choose favourite sleeping spots. Often these will be in cool or shaded patches on a very hot day, somewhere warm and free of drafts on a cold day, and of course on a surface that is as comfortable and snuggly as possible. Cat owners have stopped being surprised to find their cat sleeping on a chair, a bed, in a draw on top of clothes, or somewhere else that is not necessarily terribly convenient for the owner.

Just like human beings, when cats sleep there is more than one type of sleep: there are periods of lighter sleep and others of much deeper sleep. Interestingly, EEG results indicate that in deep sleep there is almost as much brain activity in a cat as when it is awake.

As with many other mammals, there are also periods of REM or rapid eye movement sleep. This is also a state of deep sleep and usually the phase of sleep in which dreams occur. Do cats dream? That's impossible to determine. It seems possible, however.

2) Behaviour problems

There are a number of fairly common behavioural problems one encounters in cats including the Snowshoe on occasion. It is certainly best to try and nip any undesirable behaviour in the bud when you first start to notice them before they become entrenched and much harder to deal with.

Missing the litter box

One of these areas of difficulty is when your kitten or adult cat starts to miss the litter box. Before looking for a more complex reason begin with the more obvious ones. For instance, is the litter box dirty? Cats are very clean by nature and will not use a litter box that is dirty or too damp. Have you started using a different or new type of cat litter? It might be that your kitten or cat does not like the smell or feel of it. Cats also like their privacy. Is the litter box in a place where there is a lot of activity that is off-putting for your cat?

Most of the time, this particular behavioural issue can be explained by looking at the issues discussed above. Once the underlying cause has been addressed the problem behaviour usually stops.

Scratching

A second fairly common problem is a cat that scratches your furniture, carpets, curtains and even wallpaper. If you don't already have a scratching post, buying one must be the first thing you do. If you do have a scratching post that your cat is not using, you will have to retrain it to do so (please see chapter 6).

Excessive scratching can also cause problems for a cat as it may bleed as the skin becomes raw or if a nail tears. It has been noted that cats use scratching as a tool to demand your attention. It is best to take note of this behaviour before your Snowshoe inflicts physical pain on itself.

Urinating or defecating in the house

An unfortunately common behavioural problem with cats is urination or defecation in the house. This is a very unpleasant for cat owners in terms of knowing how to deal with their cat, cleaning up the mess, stains and the various unpleasant smells – sometimes lingering ones – that go with it.

There could be a number of reasons why your cat is doing this. With urinating, the most frequent reasons are that your cat is marking the house as his or her territory, they have a medical problem, they can't or won't use the litter box for some reason or they are stressed or frightened. Once you have ruled out a medical reason you can deal with the underlying cause and the behaviour should stop.

Remember not to shout at your cat, smack him or her or rub a cat's nose in it; this will just create a fearful, stressed cat and it will not stop the behaviour.

Attention seeking disorder

Cats with this problem will 'meow' nonstop at certain times of the day or night. Their constant howling can become a nuisance for the owner, family and even neighbours. One needs to try and understand what is causing a cat to behave in this manner. The howling of a cat can be broadly categorized as crying or meowing. The cause for such behaviour can be either emotional or physical pain that the cat is experiencing.

Some cats produce a truly mournful howl that sounds as though they are calling out for help. This particular howl can make the cat owner cringe with sympathy for the poor creature. It can be a result of pain, suddenly feeling lost, deafness or even a call for help from an old or infirm cat. Some cat owners think that it can also happen when a cat wakes from a bad dream.

The reason for this howl need not always be an emotional one. A certain condition called Feline Hyperesthesia is also associated with this distressing behaviour. When a cat howls during the night and is found rolling on the floor then you must consider this condition. This condition is more commonly known as Rippling Skin Disorder and is a stress related condition. However, the symptoms usually include a set of unrelated issues. The cats with this condition tend to become extremely sensitive to touch and the skin begins to show ripples.

The possible causes of this disorder are the excessive presence of unsaturated fatty acids in combination with Vitamin E deficiency, brain infection or trauma or even flea allergies. If the cat is diagnosed with this disorder then it is unlikely that it will be completely cured. So, paying attention to these issues can help you to provide greater comfort to the cat and monitor its behavioural issues effectively and appropriately.

Chronic pseudo hunger can also cause these upsetting howls. They are not uncommon in cats. Like people, cats also have food cravings which are unwarranted. Cats tend to develop a strong liking for some treats such as tuna flakes. This can also turn into an addiction of sorts. This causes the cat to beg for food all day because of cravings that are misread as hunger.

Cats that run in circles around their owner's feet are at risk of accidentally being trodden on and / or making their owner fall. This is also categorized under attention seeking issues in cats. They are much like children who need a little bit of extra attention. These cats also tend to rub themselves against your arm when they need want attention from you.

Cats are vocal generally and the Snowshoe is more so than many breeds. They like to have conversations with their owners. Some chatty cats tend to draw their owners into lengthy conversations. If the owner doesn't spend enough time with a cat that is very sociable and chatty, it is likely to become lonely, stressed and even depressed.

Aggression towards other cats

Many people don't get too concerned when their cats have scraps or the odd fight. An all out fight with an outsider tends to be more dramatic and taken more seriously. However, it is wise to be watchful when your cats get into a fight because you have to make sure that the fight doesn't become too serious.

Cats fight for several reasons including fear, territorial disputes or misunderstandings, competition for a female, the venting of stress, anxiety, display etc. There are various kinds of aggression that are seen in cats.

Sexual aggression in cats is a common phenomenon but it is not often seen. However, when two cats get sexually aggressive towards each other, the dominant cat bites the nape of the less dominant or the subservient cat's neck and then attempts to climb onto the subservient cat's back.

Territorial aggression is also observed quiet often amongst all animals including domestic cats. Cats mark their territory by urinating, spraying or rubbing their faces against objects. This leaves their scent, or pheromones, which tells other cats whose turf or territory it is. Cats will hiss and growl to warn an intruder that he or she is unwelcome. If the intruder pays no attention to the warnings then a fight will usually take place. Fortunately, this does not occur between Snowshoe cats too often as they are, as a rule, less territorial than most other breeds.

Aggression directed at human beings

It is unlikely that your cat will become friendly with everybody who visits your home. Most domesticated cats are civil to guests or will simply quietly leave if they are uncomfortable in their company. However, when a cat tends to get aggressive towards people in general then it is a clear indication of the fact that the particular cat has been poorly trained when it was younger. Biting, scratching and unpleasant vocalization are indications of a badly trained or unsocialised cat. Some possible causes of aggressive cat behaviour towards human beings are:

Overstimulation: This problem surfaces when the owner of the cat or a person does not understand the body language of the cat. There are cats that enjoy petting while others prefer to be left alone. Even the most petting-friendly cats don't like to be cuddled or stroked for unreasonable lengths of time or too hard. When they get over stimulated, they tend to scratch or bite to show that the petting session is over.

If one watches a cat closely you will see that the cat starts moving away. It might begin by pulling its ears back and narrowing its eyes. If the owner fails to understand these signals then the cat begins to lash its tail. Finally, if the owner continues the cat may become aggressive and scratch or bite.

Redirected aggression comes about when the cat's aggression towards his owner or other human beings is not necessarily due to something that person has done but to something else that has frightened or disturbed the cat. For example, when your Snowshoe spots a foreign cat or any other strange animal around the house there is a possibility of the cat becoming agitated and aggressive. As a reaction to this your cat will scratch or bite the first thing it can reach.

3) *Going away and travelling with your Snowshoe*

Whether you are going on a vacation or even going on a business trip, the biggest issue that you will face is making the right arrangements for your Snowshoe while you are away. You must ensure that your cat is in safe hands and is somewhere where it will be treated well and given a lot of love and affection. There are several options that are available, but the most common and the most reliable ones are:

- *Friends*: If you are a cat lover, you will in all likelihood be in the company of several others who love, even adore, cats. There will probably be someone in your group who can pitch in to take care of your cat while you are away. When you are handing this responsibility over to a friend, make sure that he or she has had pets in the past, preferably a cat. You must look for someone who will be able to make your cat comfortable and less anxious.

- *Family*: If you have relatives who visit you regularly, leaving your cat in their care is a great idea because your cat will be familiar with the smell, sound and sight of them and will be able to adjust better in their company. If someone from your family is willing to stay over at your home and take care of your cat while you are away, it is the best possible scenario.

- *A neighbour*: If you have friendly neighbours who love cats, ask them to take care of your Snowshoe. Neighbours, again, will be familiar to your cat and will therefore be able to comfort it while you are away. In addition, the locality and the surroundings will not be too different for your cat to make adjustments to.

- *A pet sitter*: There are several companies and a number of individuals who will be willing to provide you with pet sitting services while you are away. You can ask for recommendations from people who have used these services in the past to choose the right company for your Snowshoe.

You should meet the people who work at the company or the pet sitter before you appoint them. If you are sure that they are gentle, kind and, most importantly, responsible, you can do a trial run for one evening. If you see that they are good with your cat and that your cat is comfortable in their presence, you can give them the responsibility of taking care of your Snowshoe while you are away.

- *A boarding home or cattery*: There are several places where your cat will be boarded for the period that you are away. These professionals have all the necessary assistance. From people who feed and clean the cages to certified vets, you will find that all the services are provided in these shelters. Here again, you can ask for recommendations before you actually decide to place your cat in a particular shelter.

  Make a visit to these places to check their standards of hygiene. The conditions of the cages, the staff and the facilities available all play an important role in the decision that you make.

If you have to travel and leave your Snowshoe home alone, make sure that you take all the necessary steps to schedule your trip according to your cat. Plan well in advance and keep a list of options that are available to take care of your cat. Never rush these things in the last minute, as you will end up making compromises on the necessary arrangements.

One can never say when an emergency will occur. In case you have to leave suddenly, you must be able to find the best assistance for your cat's care. So, it is a good idea to make a list of people or companies who will always be willing to take care of your cat while you are away.

It is a good idea to make a list of possible contacts and keep them near your phone so you can just reach out, pick the phone and make sure your cat has a safe home to stay in.

Sadly, cats are not the best travel companions. If you have had a dog for a pet, never assume that your Snowshoe will be as easy to travel with. Whether you are travelling by car or train, make sure air conditioning is available to keep your cat comfortable.

Travelling by car

If you are travelling by car, remember that you must never leave your cat to wander around in the car. If your cat jumps on the driver or gets under his or her feet or the pedals, the consequences could be fatal! Make sure that you always carry your cat in a carrier. The carrier should be extremely sturdy and must be made from metallic wires or even fibre glass. The carriers made from light plastic or even cardboard are not meant for long journeys. They are only suitable for short trips like a visit to the vet.

The weather that you travel in is extremely important in deciding what measures you need to take while travelling. If you think that it will get hotter as you proceed, make sure that you get a carrier that allows a good amount of air circulation. In case it is going to get cold along the way, carry enough blankets to wrap your Snowshoe up and keep it warm. There are also draft free carriers that will ensure that you do not leave your kitty shivering and uncomfortable.

Irrespective of the kind of carrier that you buy, there is one more thing that you need to consider. In case you are planning to change your mode of transport along the way, plane for example, you must also check the guidelines that they provide with respect to the type of carrier that is allowed.

If you have ample space in the back of your car and you only intend to travel by car, you can even use a large crate to keep your cat in. All you need to do is place blankets and sheets inside this crate and put it in the back of your car. The only thing that you need to ensure is that you provide your cat with a quiet place where he can rest during the journey. Place his favourite toys and treats around him to reduce the stress of travelling. The bedding that you provide during the travelling period should be what he or she is already used to.

Make sure that the crate or the carrier is completely secure. Even if you were to apply brakes suddenly it must be safe. If the carrier or crate falls suddenly or slides forward, your Snowshoe will be startled and might even be hurt. The last thing you want while travelling is an anxious or injured cat.

Finally, never allow the cat to be placed in the boot as this area is very dark and badly ventilated. Check on your cat regularly throughout the journey and make sure that it is comfortable.

Travelling by train

When you are travelling by train you must obviously place your cat in a carrier. Since there are several strangers on a train, you do not want to have any instances of your cat breaking free and running scared or scaring the passengers. So, make sure that the carrier that you have is extremely sturdy.

The base of the carrier must be strong to ensure that your cat is secured. The carrier itself should be light so that you do not have any difficulty carrying it around. It must also be of a convenient size depending upon the space available on the train. Make sure that you get a carrier that is large enough for your cat to rest in. Never cram your Snowshoe into a small carrier because there isn't enough storage space.

You must keep a familiar blanket in the carrier to reduce anxiety. However, littering and soiling can be quite a concern. So, line your cat's cage with a good amount of absorbent paper so that you both have a pleasant journey.

Travelling by Air

Travelling with your pet by air requires a good deal of planning in advance. Not all airlines are prepared to transport cats. If they do, they are usually handled as freight. However, if you do find airlines that have the facility to transport your Snowshoe, you must take several precautions. For instance, don't ever transport a pregnant cat or a kitten that is younger than three months of age by air.

Check on the necessity for a license to transport animals in the airlines that you choose. Furthermore, there are chances that you and your cat will travel on separate flights. If this will be the case, you should make sure that you get a direct flight for your cat so that he or she does not have to deal with additional stressors and an even longer journey because of issues such as transits and transfers.

Find out what type of proof of vaccinations and health status you need to provide. Some airline companies also insist that a cat that is going into the cargo hold must be sedated for the duration of the flight.

Travelling with your Snowshoe can be fun if you prepare it in advance. The most important thing to do is to condition him or her to enjoy sitting inside a carrier. If you are able to accomplish this, you have already won half the battle.

4) Why and how your cat purrs

It used to be believed that cats purr when they are content and happy. This is only part of what is apparently a far more complex and fascinating mechanism. Research now indicates that it is a means of communicating and may also be a form of self-healing.

A cat will also purr if it feels threatened or frightened. A vet by the name of Kelly Morgan has an interesting theory: a purr is the feline equivalent of a smile in people. This makes sense as people smile when happy, sometimes to hide embarrassment, to appease the other person or even to mask anger.

How a cat purrs is also interesting. A part of the brain, a neural oscillator, sends a message to the muscles of the larynx. These muscles begin to twitch incredibly fast: 25 – 150 vibrations per second. Because of the vibrations, the vocal cords separate as the cat breathes in and out. The resulting sound is a purr.

In addition to using the purr to communicate with people and perhaps each other, bioacoustics researchers now think that purring helps cats to heal. Vibrations in the range that the vocal cords vibrate have been shown to relieve pain, heal wounds faster and even promote bone growth and increase bone density. The purring of your Snowshoe could well have health and healing benefits for you too.

5) Feline stress and dealing with it

Animals also get stressed, as people do, but they don't have the same range of options to relieve their stress that we do. Your Snowshoe will lower your stress levels. You need to do the same for him or her!

Stress has its advantages because, thanks to the adrenaline it releases, it can boost performance or even help an animal, and people, avoid injury or death. It is responsible for the important "Fight or flight" response. The danger arises when the stress is either acute or chronic; if we or a cat goes on feeling stressed for a long time there are numerous harmful effects.

The most significant of the physical consequences is damage to the immune system. A chronically stressed cat can lose its appetite, become agitated, urinate or defecate in the house, spray, begin to tremble or shiver, cry much more than usual, become very restless or even hide. Keep in mind, though, that these symptoms could also be caused be a medical condition so you need to rule that possibility out first by having a vet check your cat.

Once you know that your Snowshoe isn't sick, you need to identify the stressor or cause of the stress. Have you moved recently? Has a new pet or person been introduced into your home? Is there new furniture or have you redecorated? Are you packing to go away? Has your neighbour acquired a new pet that your cat could have had contact with? Any of these changes, or a host of others, could stress some cats. Others will take it in their stride or find it fun!

Your first line of attack is to change the situation that is causing the problem. If that is not going to be possible you may need to consider removing the cat. For instance, if there are workmen in your home consider placing your Snowshoe with a trusted friend or at a cattery until your home is back to normal.

The next option is to help your cat change its response to stress. Spend extra time with your Snowshoe stroking and soothing it. Massaging cats can have a wonderfully relaxing effect on them (and you). Stroke and speak to your cat as you slowly approach the source of stress.

Don't push too hard or rush your cat; you need to acclimatize him or her gently. If necessary you can get a sedative of some sort from the vet to take the edge off the anxiety. In extreme cases some owners opt to consult a cat therapist.

6) *Moving house with your cat*

Moving house with a Snowshoe is easier than with many other breeds because they are less territorial than most and, so long as you are around, your cat should cope fairly well. However, there are still things that you need to do – or not do – to make a move as non-stressful as possible.

If you are just moving a short distance, say within the same city or town, you need to move your belongings and set up your new home first before you move your cat. That way, you can arrive with your cat in its carrier and introduce it to the new house with the familiar furniture already in place.

However, if you are moving a greater distance you will need to transport your cat in your car or on a train or plane as discussed and described in detail earlier in this chapter. Remember to always use your cat's own blanket and a toy or two for the comfort of familiar scents and objects.

If you are still arranging furniture or the movers are still moving in and out of the premises when you arrive, you must try to spare your Snowshoe all, or most of, of the commotion and upheaval. Find a quiet, safe room in the new house where you can put him or her. Leave the carrier, a blanket, food, water and a litter box in the room. Keep the door closed or locked so he or she won't be bothered or accidently let out of the room. Remember to visit your cat regularly and make some time to pet and talk to it.

When you move into a new home you need to keep your Snowshoe inside even if ordinarily he or she was allowed outside at your previous home. This is a new and therefore unknown and scary environment for your cat. A real danger can be if a cat gets a fright or becomes alarmed and it is not yet familiar with its surroundings. It could run and either get lost or encounter trouble in the form of other animals or traffic in nearby roads. Your cat must, even if only initially, be a purely inside cat until you are sure that he or she is completely settled.

Of course there will be some variation from cat to cat. Some cats will settle fast and will be able – and want – to explore the whole house from the start. Others will need a room or a hiding place in which to settle and they will venture out for short exploratory trips until they are confident enough to look the whole place over. Then there are other cats, including many Snowshoe cats, who will settle pretty quickly so long as their owner is there. Of course there are also cats that will only emerge from hiding after being bribed, cajoled and begged.

Some cat owners find it helpful to go on a tour of the new house with their cat. If your cat is too nervous to follow you or walk with you, you could pick him or her up and do the tour together. Again, make sure to speak soothingly to your Snowshoe and pet him or her so it knows all is well.

As a rule, if your furniture is in place and most smells are familiar your cat will settle in well and make the necessary adjustments. If, however, your cat is of a generally more nervous disposition it might not be a bad idea to speak to your vet about a mild sedative to help your Snowshoe make the move more easily and with less stress.

Chapter 11: Becoming a Snowshoe breeder

If you want to breed Snowshoe cats you will need several things in addition to a passion for it: a vet who you have a good relationship with and who understands and knows the breed, lots of available time, energy, a mentor or advisor such as an established breeder, the ability to deal with some heartache and the necessary money. If you only want to breed the Snowshoe because you have heard there are waiting lists for them and money to be made, you are in the wrong business!

As a breeder you will need to be even more hygiene and health conscious than you are as a cat owner. The kittens especially are vulnerable when they are very young and can be prone to respiratory illnesses. In fact, one of your responsibilities will be to learn about cat illnesses. You need to read a lot, talk to vets and or breeders and get as much information as you can so that you can pick up signs or symptoms early. In other words, a breeder must know about illnesses, transmission, prevention and treatment.

It is also advisable to become a registered breeder. Find out from an Internet search, your mentor, an existing breeder or your vet which associations you need to investigate and join. Membership gives you access to really useful information and a support network. It also gives you credibility as a breeder in the eyes of people who will buy kittens or cats from you.

There are also numerous very helpful – and often fun – blogs, newsletters, clubs, forums and chat rooms out there that focus on the Snowshoe breed. Have a look at them, join or follow them or subscribe to newsletters and decide which you find useful or just enjoyable. It can be very productive to spend time in chat rooms or open blogs where Snowshoe breeders and owners share experiences and offer comments or advice.

1) Sexual maturity

If you buy a registered Snowshoe kitten with a view to becoming a breeder you need to know when it is sexually mature and at what age you can start to breed with it.

Both males (toms) and females (queens) usually reach puberty at around 6 months. However, as with humans there are always some variations. Some cats reach sexual maturity as early as 4 months. On the other hand, some females are only ready at about a year. You will have to establish the status or sexual maturity of your cat by its behaviour.

Females will come onto heat. When she does you will notice that she is far more affectionate and vocal than usual. She may also yowl to attract a mate. You need to keep your very young female inside and safe because you don't want her to get pregnant by a non Snowshoe or when she is still too young to safely have a litter.

Males that are sexually mature will also become far more vocal. They will try to get out and may also spray to mark territory and attract a female. Here again you need to keep your male cat inside until the urge to mate subsides.

Females should not be used for breeding until they are 18 to 24 months old. Males should not be used until they are 18 months old. You want a cat that is not only sexually mature but also fully grown, strong and more grown up.

2) Breeding: general pointers

The single most important activity is monitoring a female's heat cycle very carefully. When a cat is in heat, 1 or 2 eggs are released by the ovaries in a 24 hour period. If your cat's heat lasts 7 days that's 7 to 14 eggs. So, a female cat that mates each of those 5 days could well conceive on each day.

Given a week in a cat pregnancy is like a month for a human one, the kitten(s) conceived on day 7 will be born at the same time as the kitten(s) conceived on day 1. The day 7 kitten is effectively premature (in human terms it is a month premature) and therefore vulnerable to a number of potentially fatal health problems.

The solution is pretty simple: only allow your female to mate during the first half (2 or 3 days) of the heat cycle. That way all the kittens will be developed to almost identical stages and you will greatly reduce the chance of loosing kittens.

The interval between one heat cycle and another is usually about 10 days. You therefore should expect your female cat to exhibit this behaviour at least twice in a month during the breeding season.

The hormonal changes that take place in the cat's body in this period are tremendous. While oestrogen causes the onset of the heat cycle, progesterone takes over when she is pregnant. As the level of oestrogen increases, the heat cycle will intensify. Once the level of oestrogen drops, the heat cycle ends. This rise and fall of oestrogen will only end when she is mated.

The mating season usually starts in January or February and continues until October or. The temperature during this season and the ratio between light and dark hours will play a significant role in your cat's heat cycle.

3) Finding the right mate

Cats are extremely sensitive creatures. Most often, they will be able to choose their own mates when you take them to the breeder. If your cat has not been neutered or spayed, make sure you take them to a good breeder, especially with a pedigreed cat like the Snowshoe.

For Snowshoe cats it is now necessary for you to pick another Snowshoe for mating as out crossing is now very strictly controlled. Given the goal is to achieve the Snowshoe physical characteristics and a healthy litter, a pure parent breed is recommended.

You must always take a queen to the tom for breeding, as she will not be too sensitive to these environmental changes during the mating process. The actual mating does not last for more than 4 minutes. Once this is over, the queen will break free by striking the male with her paw and turning away. The after-reaction of the female is cleaning herself after rolling and thrashing for a while. The after-reaction may last up to 9 minutes.

If you are interested in producing a litter, you may have to allow your cat to be mated multiple times. With a single mating, there is only a 50% chance of your cat getting pregnant. Studies show that female cats will allow up to 30 matings at intervals of 5 minutes.

One interesting fact about cats in general is that while each kitten has one father, the fathers of the kittens in a single litter may not have the same father. This is true because of the multiple mating processes. Of course this will not be the case if the queen is only covered by one tom.

Once the kittens arrive you also need to make sure both mother and babies are kept at the right temperature. You must keep the basket or nesting place out of drafts as kittens are prone to respiratory problems when they are very little. They aren't able to regulate their body temperature the way the adults can. If they get too cold they can't digest their milk or get the nutrients they need.

4) *What to feed your pregnant cat*

The most important rule is to continue to feed your pregnant Snowshoe a healthy and balanced diet. A pregnant cat may ask for extra food but you need to be strong and resist her pleas; extra food will result in weight gain, which will be bad for her as it puts stress on the organs. This in turn is unhealthy for the unborn kittens.

Some vets recommend a diet that contains calcium, phosphorus and extra protein. It's also suggested that several small meals throughout the day is better for a pregnant cat that two larger meals each day.

5) Gestation

For the first 3 to 4 weeks one often doesn't notice anything about the cat's condition. You will probably spot behaviour changes first. A pregnant cat will become even more home loving and will probably start to sleep more. She often also becomes increasingly affectionate and demonstrative towards her owners and will actively look for attention to a marked degree.

By the 16th day of pregnancy the rounded abdomen should make it obvious that your cat is pregnant. If you are not experienced with cats, an ultrasound can help you decide if your cat is pregnant or not. There is an easy way to check. If the uterus feels stringy, it means that your cat might be pregnant. By the 20th day of pregnancy, you can actually feel the kitten foetuses in the abdomen of the queen when she is relaxed.

In the fourth week of pregnancy the nipples or teats will start to become a darker pink and to protrude. In the fifth week you will notice that her tummy gradually gets rounder. The standard gestation period for cats is 62 to 65 days. There is some variation by a day or two on either side.

About two weeks, sometimes one, before the kittens are due the mother will begin to look for a suitable place in which to give birth. It's not a bad idea to provide a basket or a box with a towel or blanket in it in a place that is peaceful and warm.

The box or basket must be of sufficient size to allow the cat to stretch out full length. Of course in typical cat fashion you will know soon enough if what you have provided is not what she wants! Your cat may go off and select a draw or cupboard or somewhere else that is not ideal from your point of view but certainly is from hers.

Besides checking for pregnancy, ultrasound is also a useful tool to establish whether or not the development of the foetuses is normal. You can have an ultrasound performed by your vet from the 26th day of pregnancy onwards.

6) Special care for a pregnant cat

The pregnancy period is a very delicate one. You must ensure that you take the best care of your Snowshoe so that she stays well, produces a healthy litter and has a safe and, hopefully, easy delivery.

There are a few things to keep in mind while caring for a pregnant cat:

- ✓ Morning sickness is very common in cats. Your vet will be able to provide you with assistance if this persists or is severe.
- ✓ Your pregnant cat may also reduce her food consumption by the third week of pregnancy.
- ✓ Overfeeding and weight gain during pregnancy can lead to complications during labour so resist giving her extra food or meals.
- ✓ The food that you give your pregnant queen must be highly nutritious.
- ✓ Protein and calcium are a must in her diet. However, never provide any supplements unless recommended by a vet.
- ✓ Your cat should be kept indoors during the last 15 days of pregnancy. This helps you ensure that she does not give birth elsewhere.
- ✓ During your cat's pregnancy, you must make sure that you take her to visit the vet for regular check-ups. The most important time for your vets visit is during the last two weeks of pregnancy.

In addition to this, you should continue with the usual grooming routine and lavish her with love, affection and praise.

7) Preparing for and assisting at the birth

There are a few things that you should keep handy when your Snowshoe is in the last two weeks of her pregnancy:

- A sturdy box of some sort
- Surgical gloves
- Syringe or eyedropper to remove secretions from the nose and mouth.
- Cotton thread or Dental floss for the umbilical cord ties
- Antiseptic for the umbilical stumps
- Sharp, clean scissors
- Clean and fresh towels
- The vet's number
- Emergency contact numbers.

Now all you need to do is prepare for the actual birth. When your cat is in the last week of her pregnancy, place the kittening box in a quiet spot. This spot should be warm and completely draft free. Place your cat's favourite blanket and some toys in this box to encourage her to sleep there before the kittens are born. The bedding that you choose should be comfortable for the kittens and shouldn't snag their claws. The bedding must be changed and washed regularly after the birth.

Danger signs

If you observe one or more of the following symptoms during your cat's pregnancy or the delivery you must contact your vet right away:

- Lack of appetite in your queen for 24 hours or more
- Your cat's temperature is high and continues to stay elevated
- She becomes lethargic and lacks interest in anything
- There is an unpleasant smelling discharge from the vagina.

These are all signs that something might have gone wrong during the gestation or delivery. If it is after the birth they probably indicate post natal stress in your cat and they must be treated at the earliest opportunity.

Things not to do during pregnancy

- Never use any flea powder or medicine without consulting your vet first.
- Don't give your Snowshoe medication without a valid prescription.
- Do not use antiseptics suitable for humans. These products may burn your cat's delicate skin.
- Avoid handling the kittens too much. There is a chance that a mother cat will disown or even kill the kittens if they are threatened by intruders. Allow the kittens and the mother to bond.
- Allow your cat to roam around. Cats can get pregnant within 2 weeks of delivery. So keep her in confinement for a while.
- Have your cat sterilised in the 7 weeks after the kittens' birth.

Taking care of a pregnant cat is a huge responsibility. If you are not sure how to go about it, you can look for a shelter or a veterinary hospital where the cat will be taken care of until the kittens are born. Once the kittens have been born, you can decide if you want to keep them in your home or find them another loving home to live in.

8) The birth itself

You will notice that your pregnant cat starts to become rather restless at about 12 or 24 hours before she's going to give birth. She will go back and inspect the nesting place several times, sometimes adjusting the bedding. At this point she will probably also stop eating.

The first sign that the birth is imminent is that there will be a slight discharge of clear amniotic fluid. This is the feline equivalent of water breaking. As with human beings and other animals, contractions will become stronger and closer together over time. There is no hard and fast rule about how your cat will behave while she is in labour. Cats with very strong bonds to their humans, like the Snowshoe, will probably not want to be left on their own. However, more experienced mothers are quite happy to get on with it on their own in peace and quiet.

Once the cervix has opened, expulsion contractions begin. The cat will usually lie on her side or even squat, using her stomach muscles to assist the contractions. After this point the birth of the kittens occurs rapidly. Most kittens are born headfirst but almost a third of kittens are breech births with the hindquarters appearing first.

When the kitten has been born the mother will tear the amniotic sac open if it hasn't already broken. She will drink the fluid and eat the sac and then begin to lick and clean the kitten. This licking not only cleans and dries the kitten but it also stimulates the newborn's circulation and respiration.

Once all the kittens have been born the placenta is discharged or removed and eaten by the mother. If the umbilical cord has not already detached from each kitten, the mother will nibble gently through it.

The reason the mother disposes of the amniotic sac, fluid and placenta is to keep her nest clean, prevent smells and it also provides her with high quality, energy boosting food.

9) Dealing with the umbilical cord if the mother doesn't

In the unlikely event that the mother does not sever the umbilical cord herself you must do so. It's very important to remember that you need to wait 5 to 10 minutes before severing the cord. If you don't there is a risk that the kitten will suffer brain damage. This is as a result of depriving the kitten of maximum blood supply during the crucial first few minutes after birth.

Before cutting the cord, apply a ligature by tying a piece of thread or dental floss that has been soaked in disinfectant solution around the umbilical cord about 2 cm (3/4") from the kitten's body. Cut the cord with disinfected scissors 1 cm (1/3") from the ligature on the side of the placenta, not the kitten. Then you need to clean the cut end of the cord with tincture of iodine or some other disinfectant solution.

10) Feeding kittens if the mother can't or shouldn't

Sometimes a kitten has to be hand fed because the mother has died, has no milk or rejects the kitten or the kitten is too weak to suckle.

You can either purchase a kitten formula from your vet or you can make up your own. The first do-it-yourself formula contains 1 cup evaporated or powdered milk mixed with boiled water and made up to double the strength recommended for human babies. Add to the mix one egg yolk and 1 teaspoon of glucose additive. The second option is to use half a cup of cow's milk mixed with an egg yolk and 1 teaspoon of glucose. If the kitten gets diarrhoea, you need to dilute the mixture further.

Before you begin to feed the kitten, make sure that the substitute milk is body temperature. During the first week of life a kitten requires about 5 ml or 1 teaspoon of milk substitute every two hours. Thereafter the frequency of feedings should be decreased and the amount of milk substitute increased. Four hourly feeding is sufficient once the kitten has reached the age of 2 weeks.

There are two methods that can be used to feed a kitten. Firstly one can do bottle feeding. With this method you should hold the kitten firmly but gently with its head elevated slightly. Move the teat of the bottle in and out of the kitten's mouth and express a small amount of milk to encourage the kitten to develop a sucking response. If you are dealing with a very small and weak kitten you may need to resort to stomach tube feeding. It is strongly recommended that you consult your local vet for a demonstration of the correct way to do this so that no damage is accidentally done to the oesophagus or any other internal organs or tissue.

Chapter 12: The aging Snowshoe cat

1) The ageing Snowshoe

As with any other species, humans included, aging brings an increasing number of health problems and general deterioration. The ageing process can't be stopped, but there are some things we can do to minimise the effects and to make a cat's life as happy and comfortable as possible.

Age related changes

The changes you will see in your cat include:

- *Claws*: while some body processes are slowing down, cat's claws actually grow faster as they get older so it is necessary to trim their nails more frequently.

- *Feeding and drinking*: an older cat may experience a loss of appetite or be reluctant to eat. If he or she is experiencing problems with their teeth or gums this could also cause difficulty. Older cats also feel thirsty more often than younger cats.

- *Digestive problems*: your cat may not be able to process food the way it did or tolerate the same kinds of food it did when it was younger. To deal with these issues it can be helpful to feed your cat three or four small meals a day, increase the amount of moist foods in the diet or move to special or prescription food. Your vet will be able to advise you about the best one for your Snowshoe.

- *Sleep*: ageing cats will want and need to sleep even more than their younger counterparts. In addition, their sleep is often deeper and your cat is likely to be very startled if woken suddenly. Wherever possible, allow your elderly feline friend to sleep quietly and undisturbed.

- *Weight loss*: this often occurs gradually – over a period of several months – and you might not even notice this change in your cat at first. The weight loss occurs even when the cat continues to eat well.

- *Joint changes*: arthritis and osteoarthritis will cause your cat to move stiffly when he or she first gets or wakes up. In more the advanced stages of these conditions, a cat may have difficulty walking and jumping up onto surfaces such as beds and chairs. As soon as you notice these symptoms in your Snowshoe, take him or her to the vet for treatment or at least symptomatic and pain relief.

- *Constipation*: if your cat is an outdoors cat, you may not notice that he or she is having this difficulty. It is important, however, not to allow constipation to continue as it could result in a potentially dangerous bowel blockage or obstruction. Cat laxative products are available from vets some of which can be added to the cat's food. Many vets caution against the use of medicinal paraffin for cats.

- *Blindness*: usually a cat's eye sight will deteriorate gradually. Signs to look out for are white patches near the centre of the eye or a bluish, slightly opaque film over the eye. Once the cat's eyesight has become a really bad you will notice him or her starting to walk into furniture and showing reluctance to go out. All you can do is take steps to protect your cat from obvious dangers like stairs and swimming pools and not change the environment, for instance don't move furniture around.

- *Deafness*: like failing eyesight, loss of hearing also usually happens over an extended period of time. It may take a while for you to notice that your Snowshoe does not respond to noises or to being called. This makes them more at risk if they are outdoors as they won't hear other animals or cars approaching.

- *Senility*: if your cat suffers from this condition you will notice that he or she will seem particularly restless and disorientated. There may also be increased meowing or crying and demand for your attention as your cat seeks comfort and reassurance. In other words, even your Snowshoe will want more attention than usual. You need to be patient, loving and understanding and involve your vet as and when necessary.

2) How to make your aging Snowshoe comfortable

While you can do very little about some of the symptoms and problems your cat will face, there are certain things you can do to reduce your cat's discomfort and stress.

Firstly, monitor your cat's food and drink intake. If necessary, heat your cat's food slightly to encourage it to eat. Alternatively, introduce something new into the diet. If your cat is being very inactive and sleeping a great deal you need to decrease its food intake slightly. If you don't, he or she will put on weight and this can lead to other health problems. Also, if possible, be aware of bowel activity and urination.

Secondly, place your cat's bed and bedding in a quiet spot that is not in direct sun and drafts and where it is fairly close to the litter box if your Snowshoe is using one.

Next, you should accompany your elderly cat into outdoor areas or other places where he or she may encounter difficulties or dangers, especially if your cat has poor vision and / or hearing. This helps to protect it from possible accidents and decreases the cat's stress levels.

Finally, take your aging cat to the vet for regular check-ups and monitoring. You also need to maintain vaccinations and all the standard health and hygiene routines.

3) How do you know it's time to let go?

One response to this question that struck a cord is that it is time to say goodbye to your elderly Snowshoe companion when he or she no longer responds to you and seems to get no pleasure from life. Certainly nobody wants to see a creature they love suffering or fading away.

The Downing Centre for Animal Pain Management drew up a scale to measure animal's quality of life. The test itself was developed by a veterinary oncologist. The criteria the test uses are: pain levels, the ability to eat enough to prevent hunger or malnutrition, the ability to drink and stay hydrated, the ability to groom or be groomed and the cat's ability to move around or be mobile. In other words, the scale looks at pain levels, appetite and the ability to eat, the ability to drink, whether the cat can still groom itself, if there is evidence that the cat can still enjoy activities and interactions with people and other animals, that he or she can walk or move around with relative ease and, finally, if the cat has more days that are good than ones that are bad.

Each criterion should be rated on a scale of 1 to 10 with 10 being ideal, for example pain-free would be 10. If your cat scores more than 35 then its quality of life is still acceptable. A score below that and you need to start considering euthanasia.

Chapter 13: Prices and costs

1) How to choose a breeder

Taking the time to do some research to find good and reputable Snowshoe breeders is well worth it. A good place to start is with cat registries such as TICA or CFA. The various cat associations also offer breeder lists on their websites. In fact, the more investigating you do and the more people you talk to the better.

In addition to being able to find breeders details on the Internet, you will also be able to locate the "bad breeder list". Knowing which breeder not to go to is as useful as knowing which ones to approach. You could also join Snowshoe forums online and follow or contribute to blogs. Chatting to Snowshoe owners could also provide you with very valuable information.

How do you recognize a reputable breeder? There is no way of choosing a breeder that is 100% safe or fool proof, but there are some things that you can look out for. A reputable breeder:

- Will be able to show you references
- Won't sell kittens younger than 12 weeks old
- Will show you around his or her facility
- Won't have multiple litters available at the same time
- Will be able to provide proof of vaccinations and so on
- Won't sell kittens to pet stores
- Will breed using pedigreed cats and cat prove it
- Won't sell kittens for a far lower price than the average
- Will offer a health guarantee on kittens.

Taking time to select the right breeder is a crucial first step in finding a healthy Snowshoe that is right for you. Don't rush.

2) *The cost to purchase a Snowshoe cat or kitten*

The price of Snowshoe kittens varies from breeder to breeder and from country to country. Even within countries there can be regional differences.

At time of writing, the price range was considerable. Some breeders charge $500 or £290 per kitten and those that sell highly pedigreed kittens born to show parents and that have all the necessary paperwork can sell for as much as $3000 or £1750.

Although it is unlikely, a Snowshoe kitten might be found at a shelter. In this event the price will of course be far less.

A word of caution: if you see kittens advertised for less than $500 or £290 each they are may well be the products of 'kitten mills' and should be avoided. The so-called breeder should be reported to your local cat or Snowshoe association and an animal welfare organization.

3) *Monthly costs of caring for your cat*

Monthly costs will clearly be determined by a wide range of factors including your location, your choice of brands and products, your kitten or cat's age and its state of health. If you own a Snowshoe you need to be able to accommodate the following regular expenses:

✓ Good quality cat food
✓ Grooming products
✓ Vaccination and deworming costs
✓ Cat litter
✓ Toys
✓ Food and water bowls
✓ Treats
✓ (Sometimes high) vet bills following illness or injury
✓ Pet insurance (optional).

Once-off expenses will include registration (if necessary), having your Snowshoe spayed or neutered, micro-chipping and a cat carrier.

There are also items that will have to be replaced from time to time such as beds and bedding, scratching posts, toys and food and water bowls.

The once-off costs, at time of writing, were in the region of:

- A litter box: $3-20 / £3-28
- Carrier: $20-50 / £15-45
- Toys: average $3 / £2.50 each
- Food and water bowls: $4-10 / £1-10
- Scratch post: $ / £4-110

Monthly costs were:

- Food: $17 / £15
- Cat litter: $10 / £12
- Grooming and flea control: $10 / £8
- Vet: $28 / £32 (based on vaccines and annual check-up) Total: $65 / £67

Owning a pet is a big financial responsibility. It is as good as having a baby at home. If you think that you might have to compromise on any of the expenses mentioned above, make sure you re-think your decision of bringing home a Snowshoe. Having a Snowshoe will involve costs but everybody who owns one of these cats feels that it is money well spent.

4) The option to take out Pet Insurance

If you give your Snowshoe the right diet, perform all the necessary grooming and dental care and get vaccinations done as and when required, your cat should stay pretty healthy. Of course, no cat is completely safe from illness and even the healthiest cat can be injured. Cats are also living longer now and so they suffer from illnesses associated with age. In addition, vet care is becoming more expensive.

Enter pet insurance. Depending on where you are you may be able to opt to take out one of several types of cover to help you with bills when your cat needs medical care. Some insurers offer the choice of a plan that covers expenses in the event of an accident only. Others will pay costs for both accident and illness. The third option, one that usually gets added onto one of the others, is to cover routine procedures and costs such as vaccinations, deworming, dental descaling and sterilisations.

Like most insurance, these policies will have a deductible or excess that you will have to pay, but they can help greatly if your Snowshoe ever requires significant or ongoing treatment or vet care. The premium and affordability will also vary depending on the type of cover chosen and how many pets you place on the policy.

Your vet should be able to supply you with a brochure, pamphlet or information. You will have to weigh the cost of insurance against the possibility of being out of pocket at a later date.

Chapter 14: General advice & tips

Mistakes made by new Snowshoe owners

If you have just got yourself a Snowshoe cat you must make its maintenance and safety your priority. When you bring home a new cat, you get so caught up in settling it in and then playing with and petting it that you can lose sight of some important aspects. There are in fact several mistakes that new cat owners make.

If you take cat care too lightly, there is a chance that your cat will not be happy and satisfied in your home. Here are some of the most concerning mistakes a Snowshoe owner could make:

Underestimating the cost of owning a cat

Of course, bringing home a cat is not as expensive as bringing home a dog. This, however, does not mean that it is easy to have a cat at home. The expenses of taking care of the cat, its health and also the facilities that it requires can be significant.

In addition to that, cats are a big responsibility. You will have to think twice before you plan a vacation or holiday. You will have to plan your entire schedule around your Snowshoe. If you are unable or unwilling to do that, owning a cat could be a serious problem for you.

Ignoring visits to the vet

You must make sure that you make a schedule of all the necessary visits to the veterinarian. If you neglect to do so there is a good chance that your cat may not get the necessary vaccinations on time or at all. In addition, you might not notice the symptoms and signs of potentially hazardous diseases. Going to the vet will also help you understand if your routine with your cat is correct or not.

In case you need to make changes in the diet, tooth care or other grooming or the amount of exercise that your cat gets, your vet can provide you with the assistance you require before problems occur.

Failure to spay or neuter your Snowshoe

Breeding or mating is not the easiest thing to do with cats. In case you have ignored spaying or neutering, you will find your home in a mess during the time that your cat is in heat. It is common for male Snowshoe cats to want to roam. Female cats, on the other hand, will keep the entire household on their feet with constant purring and yowling when they are in heat.

The worst thing that can happen to you is a litter of kittens when you are not prepared for. Being unable to care for a pregnant cat or the kittens can be very stressful for you and your cat.

Buying cheap cat food

If you try to save money on cat food remember that you will probably end up paying a great deal more to help your cat recover from nutrition related health issues. Remember that the cat food you select must be a good source of proteins, vitamins and minerals. If you are unable to do that, your Snowshoe will be malnourished and unhealthy.

Cheaper varieties of cat food will only be able to provide your cat with plant based proteins. For an animal that is a carnivore, the only good source of protein is animal protein. In addition to this, the cheap pet foods contain large amounts of carbohydrates that can make your cat obese or diabetic. Make sure you only bring home high quality foods for your pet.

Allowing your cat to roam outside

By nature, a Snowshoe likes to stay indoors. If you let it loose outside there are chances that he or she will eat food or substances that are poisonous or hazardous to his or her health. Your cat may also be attacked by bigger animals and get hurt or infected.

Domesticated cats are not aggressive or defensive enough to take care of themselves in the great outdoors.

It is true that your cat will get a lot of exercise outside. However, unsupervised visits outside the house are not recommended.

Neglecting litter box hygiene

Cats are very fussy about hygiene. If you do not clean the litter box regularly you will notice peculiar behaviour patterns like littering in other places inside the house. Some cats will also not eat well if the litter box hygiene is not maintained appropriately. Examine the litter box daily and ensure that the litter is replaced on a regular basis.

Thinking your Snowshoe is a human being

No matter how intelligent, loving, funny and so on your cat is she or he is... a cat. Conversely, your cat may well view you as a large not terribly athletic cat. This means that you have to try and view things from your cat's point of view. Your cat will have a reason for doing the things it does. It's part of the cat owner's job to work out what those reasons are.

Hitting your Snowshoe

Don't ever hit your cat. There is never anything positive to be gained from this. Although they are intelligent creatures, you can't be sure that your cat will know why it is being smacked. The result you are likely to have is a cat that becomes fearful of you and anxious.

If you need to discipline your cat, do so when you catch it 'in the act'. You can clap your hands, use a firm tone when saying "No" or even spray the cat lightly with water.

Conclusion

The Snowshoe is a unique creature. This breed is elegant, vocal, very intelligent, affectionate, playful and loving. It needs attention and company and will be miserable without it. The Snowshoe also gets on well with other animals, both dogs and cats, and with children and people in general.

It is also curious—like most cats—and this combined with the high level of intelligence found in this breed mean that it is an active and energetic cat. But, it is also well behaved and easy to handle and loves to be with and please its owner. It will be a loving, loyal and robust companion to you for many years.

Balanced against these advantages is the fact that the Snowshoe is fairly energy intensive because of its need for affection and activity. If you own one of these cats you must spend a standard amount of time on grooming but a lot on cuddle and play time. If you can't do this, or are not prepared to do so, don't get a Snowshoe. In fact, you should probably reconsider getting a cat at all. They are also a fairly vocal breed so if you will be annoyed by cat-chat, chirps, trills and other kitty communication this is not the breed for you.

In other words, if you want a cat that is docile, quiet and very independent then the Snowshoe is not for you. If, on the other hand, you want a cat that is smart, energetic, gregarious and doting then there is probably no better breed for you!

If you already have a Snowshoe in your life I hope you have gained some useful new information and insights. If you were undecided about the breed I hope you are closer to a decision. If you are going to buy a Snowshoe, I hope the information here helps to prepare you!

Here is a final checklist to make sure you do not miss anything and do your best for your cat:

- Keep an eye on your pet. Be sensitive to the changes that your cat undergoes physically and mentally.
- Adapt your home so that your Snowshoe is never in danger or feels threatened.
- Treat him or her like the centre of your universe. The Snowshoe is not forgiving if it is ignored or neglected and may become stressed or even depressed.
- Make time to play: If your work comes first, do not even try to tell your Snowshoe that. They do not understand how you could possibly be too busy to play with them. Involve yourself in their playtime or you will find almost incessant meowing demolishing any chance of peace and quiet.
- Feed him or her well: Your cat is domesticated. It does not know to hunt for prey. You must keep a schedule and make sure that someone is always around to feed your cat on time. Unlike humans who would eat just about anything at any time of the day, cats are highly disciplined creatures.
- Get all the necessary identification to ensure that your Snowshoe does not end up in a shelter. Consider having your cat micro-chipped but, at the very least, get a tear-away collar with an identification disc
- Your cat's health is priority. No matter how tired or lazy you feel, you need to make sure you take your pet to the vet at the scheduled times for vaccinations, deworming, etc. Any

negligence in this area can have serious and really expensive repercussions for your Snowshoe and for you.

I hope you savour every minute of being the proud owner of a Snowshoe. With this gorgeous breed in your home, you will be the envy of your entire social circle. But above all, you have a companion who will love you as long as he or she lives.

Published by IMB Publishing 2014